Creating *Fulfilling* Relationships

Turning Cell Mates *into* Soul Mates

MICHAEL MIRDAD

GRAIL
PRESS

Creating Fulfilling Relationships
Turning Cell Mates into Soul Mates

GRAIL
PRESS

PO Box 1908
Sedona, AZ 86339
(360) 671-8349
office@GrailProductions.com
www.GrailProductions.com

Book cover and interior design by
Robert Lanphear
www.lanpheardesign.com

Back cover photo by Dasha Gaian

Library of Congress Cataloging-in-Publication Data
Mirdad, Michael.

Creating Fulfilling Relationships
Turning Cell Mates into Soul Mates/
Michael Mirdad.

Library of Congress Control Number: 2014903337
ISBN: 978-0-9855079-2-3

CONTENTS

PART ONE

Creating Fulfilling Relationships

PART TWO

Our Relationship with God: Communion

PART THREE

Our Relationship with Self: Responsibility

FOREWORD

I originally contacted Michael Mirdad when I reached out to him (knowing he had authored a book on Sacred Sexuality) to participate in the documentary *Sexology* that I was filming with my dear friend (and actress) Gabrielle Anwar. He kindly informed me that he rarely says "yes" to interviews. When I ventured to ask why he acquiesced, he replied that he could "intuitively sense that our project had integrity" and that it was "an extension of our soul's purpose." He then added that he would support our project because "the project would address more than mere sexuality; for it also addresses the wounds behind sexuality and the consequent unhealthy relationships that often follow."

Later, when I met Michael, I was touched by his humility and generosity. I had the privilege of working with him and experiencing his mastery. Out of the 44 people we interviewed, he was one of my favorites. His perspective on relationships and sexuality was candid, refreshing, deep, and respectful—all at the same time. While far too many books, teachers, and movies promote "hot sex" and pornlike behaviors, Michael said, "If sex, in and of itself, were magically transforming, there would be a lot of enlightened porn stars!" His point was that if we expect to improve our relationships and sexual experiences, we need to slow down and connect at a deeper level.

Then, in one of Michael's healing sessions, I experienced what could only be referred to as "the peace that surpasses understanding." The peace moved in waves throughout my body and felt dynamic, full of love and vitality. Then, when I experienced a counseling session with Michael, he helped me on many levels in regard to my marriage. He explained the various stages through which a relationship progresses and reminded me to "ask the right questions," rather than make assumptions, and to express my needs in the form of preferences, rather than as expectations or demands. He pointed out that the qualities we fall in love with in the beginning of our relationships are often the very things we end up disliking about our partners. This was an extremely valuable and accurate observation!

The title of this book—*Creating Fulfilling Relationships: Turning Cell Mates into Soul Mates*—reveals Michael's unique lighthearted and humorous (yet deeply profound) approach to a subject that often confounds us. He clearly and eloquently explains many of the issues that confronted, even plagued me over the course of my 16-year marriage, as well as provided the exact information that we needed for our relationship to survive. I wish that the wisdom and guidance in this book had been available to me from the beginning of my dating days. It's easy to see that many couples could benefit from this information and avoid the pitfalls and confusion that had challenged my own relationships.

I always understood intuitively that in the presence of great love, all that is less than love comes to the surface in order to be purified. It dawned on me that this is why so many relationships fall by the wayside. Once the honeymoon phase subsides, many run for the hills, disenchanted, only to recreate another infatuation. And so the cycle of superficial, evasive interaction perpetuates. Michael describes this process as the three stages of love. "If we feel love in the first stage, this love will be tried by fire in the second stage and transformed into a more authentic love that we find waiting for us in the third stage." This is a deeply meaningful revelation about the true purpose of relationship.

There was a time when I struggled in my marriage; but I came to understand that since my partner was not the main problem, I would be bound to recreate the same issues with another person if I prematurely gave up. Michael succinctly sums this up, "Relationships are for sharing love and about learning to remove all the obstacles to that love." If more people were aware of this truth, there would be far more healthy and fulfilling relationships and far less suffering.

To quote Michael again, "everything we experience in a relationship is really just a reflection of lessons and experiences within ourselves." In other words, relationship is about taking responsibility, getting to know ourselves more deeply, and finding the proper ways to create healthy communication and intimacy. Understanding that the external world is merely a reflection of our inner world is incredibly empowering.

This book is a treasure, a priceless guide to all who are committed to becoming the love they once sought to make.

Catherine Oxenberg Van Dien,
Award-winning actress and part
of the Royal Family of Yugoslavia

PREFACE

Since the beginning of time, the most perplexing of topics has been that of relationships. In fact, relationships have been on our list of things to sort out since the very first relationship on Earth, symbolized by Adam and Eve. Just when we think we have the riddle solved, the answer seems to evade us. In fact, **relationships are our most primary concern and/or struggle from the time we are born until the time we die**, which is why there have been so many books and seminars on how to "repair" relationships or how to "find the perfect partner."

This book, however, is far from a typical book on relationships. First of all, although it focuses a great deal on our relationships with others (offering numerous progressive and effective tips, insights, and exercises), this book is not *exclusively* about "romantic" relationships. Instead, **this book is about bringing *ourselves* to a healthier level so that we can create healthier relationships with *everyone*.** This book is about making *all* our relationships (not just partnerships) healthy and fulfilling. Therefore, this book focuses on how to become better people and how to create more fulfilling relationships with everyone we meet. This book encourages more reality (truth) and healthiness and less delusion and unhealthiness in our lives. After all, we are NOT merely humans having a spiritual experience; rather we are spirits having a human experience.

This book is *not* about finding yet another date or becoming attached to yet another person whom we hope will "complete us" and solve all of our problems—inside and out—only to be let down once again. **This book *is* about *Being* . . . in the Divine Love of**

God; *Feeling* . . . unconditional love within self; and *Sharing* . . . healthy love for/with others.

Like most people, I have experienced just about every type of relationship imaginable. I have had a ten-year marriage and a partnership of several years. I have shared a couple of short-term relationships of a year or so. I have had long-term and short-term "intimate friendships," and I have spent years alone, nurturing a relationship with myself. In nearly every case, my experiences have been fantastic, deep, responsible, and trusting. They have felt like truly *fulfilling* relationships. And, even though those relationships changed or ended, I actually feel love and appreciation for each person with whom I shared time and space. I am still close friends with nearly every person with whom I have shared a relationship—even going back 30 years. I've even counseled many of my former partners and friends through difficulties in their later relationships. I mention this simply to confirm that **if we nurture a healthy relationship with God (through some form of spiritual practice) and with ourselves (through self-healing and setting healthy boundaries), we can then expect to experience long-lasting and fulfilling relationships with others (when we add responsible communication and healthy acts of affection).**

Furthermore, having practiced as a spiritual counselor, as well as having taught relationship and intimacy workshops for over three decades, I have discovered ways to simplify the understanding of what seems to be a complex topic. I've also successfully taught thousands of individuals and couples how to heal their relationships of the past and how to create fulfilling relationships in the present, thus releasing the future to unlimited possibilities.

ACKNOWLEDGEMENTS

To whom do you offer thanks when you write a book on re-lationships? Everyone you have ever met? Each person I have ever met and interacted with, has, in some way, influenced who I am and where I've been. Thank you to everyone who has somehow been a part of my journey.

Many thanks to the thousands of clients, students, and friends who studied with me through one of my courses, whether the topic was specifically on relationships or merely included relation-ships as a segment.

Many thanks to my ex-wife for all her love and the many years of continued friendship (as this is the greatest proof that these princi-ples work) and to my three daughters—far into adulthood but still remembered by me as the children who used to laugh and wrestle with me and then fall asleep to my spontaneous stories and songs. I will love you girls well into the next life.

My heartfelt thanks go to Lynne Matous and Sally Richard for their superb editing. I also thank Angela, Judy, Ron, and David for their diligent proofreading and invaluable feedback. Also, thanks to Robin Rose for her artistic input and Bob Lanphear for his con-tinued brilliant book design. And special thanks go to Steve, Matt, Bruce, and all the other Spiritual Warriors who have spent lifetimes fighting for a healthier way of life.

Thanks to every teacher, counselor, and author who ever made it part of their life's purpose to assist others with their relation-ships, as there is no greater gift to bring to the world. And thanks to those who have shared *any* amount of intimate relationship with me. I truly gained from, and appreciate, each experience.

Last, but not least, I give thanks to God—the Spirit of True Love—for helping me understand relationships in a way that I might help others to find peace and joy in all of their relationships.

DISCLAIMER

The suggestions shared in this book regarding relationships and one's personal growth are merely suggestions and cannot be assumed the best options for all individuals and/or couples or for all circumstances. Therefore, although this material might work very well for some people, it is advised that each person and all couples work with the proper healers/counselors to ascertain the best plan of action for themselves and their relationships.

The contents of this book are partly from materials and transcripts of lectures and workshops Michael Mirdad has given over the last 30 years. During those years, Michael often referenced other teachers and shared some of his favorite, relevant quotes on the topic of relationships. In such cases, we have done our best to credit the sources as accurately as possible and apologize in advance if we have made any errors.

PART ONE

Creating
Fulfilling
Relationships

CHAPTER ONE

Introduction: *Creating Fulfilling Relationships*

What is the purpose of relationships? Most people seem to assume that relationships are about feeling attracted or connected to someone enough to want to spend time with them, possibly get married or commit to a partnership, and maybe even have kids and live out their years together. The reality is that most people do indeed find themselves attracted to someone and enter a relationship but, all too often, one partner usually prefers the relationship for the companionship and sex, while the other partner was hoping for companionship and a life-long relationship. Oftentimes one of them wants children, and the other is not so hot on the idea. In either case, they learn to tolerate each other; and, whether they stay together or not, they gradually grow apart in heart and soul.

Despite the countless number of books, seminars, and years of work towards finding a better way to experience relationships, the relationship struggle is still on everyone's mind and in everyone's heart. **Relationships are at the core of all that we experience in this world**. Every thought, feeling, word, and action is motivated by our relationship with God, ourselves, and/or someone else.

1

*God is known to you within relationships, as this is all that is
real here. . . It is only in relationship that anything becomes real.*
–Mari Perron and Dan Odegard

The topic of relationships is a major focus in *A Course in Miracles*.
But why would a book on spiritual psychology and the attainment
of inner peace focus on relationships? Simply because **our salva-
tion, peace of mind, and experience of unconditional love** *all*
**depend on having healed, healthy, and empowering relation-
ships.** We must learn to relate to people without attacking them or
projecting our past issues, experiences, and perceptions onto them.

But why do we have dysfunctional, codependent relationships in
the first place? It is part of our history and patterning. We believe
that we parted ways with God and, therefore, lost our connection to
our True Self and replaced it with a broken psychological self, lost
and afraid. We are then birthed into families whom we expect to
fix our brokenness, only to find that they compound our issues. We
then grew up and asked why our adult relationships seem so painful,
rather than serving as a *remedy* for life's discomforts. **We will struggle with these life-long relationship issues until we embark on
the road to healing** *and* **discover the well-spring of forgiveness.**

We never were given the chance to be anything other than the
manifestation of the fears and brokenness that we have lived with for
so long. Fortunately, there are companions we can choose to walk
with us on this road to wholeness: maybe a therapist, healer, teacher,
or even an intimate partner. It must be made clear, however, that it is
definitely wise to share the journey with *someone*—even though there
will also be times wherein we choose to walk this journey alone.

When we commit to healing our lives, we will find that we *must*
face the dark parts (false beliefs and painful memories) of our-

selves. We *can*, however, succeed in this endeavor and learn to walk through the darkness and into the light.

The truth is, however, **relationships actually have only one main purpose but with two parts: Relationships are for sharing love *and* for learning about and removing all of the obstacles *to* that love.** That's it! Every teacher, teaching, book, or workshop on relationships that fails to understand this, ends up wasting our time on the extraneous or superficial aspects of relationships. Without both healing the obstacles to love *and* nurturing the healthy means to share that love, our relationships will continue in their unhealthy cycles of false love and hate or like and dislike.

God is love, and we are made in the image of God. Therefore, *we* are love. **We were never meant to "fall in love" nor to "be in love." We were only ever meant to *be* love.** And in being love, we learn to share that love as unconditionally as possible. This is our destiny.

To develop pure and unconditional love between husband and wife, parent and child, friend and friend, self and all, is the lesson we have come to Earth to learn.

–Paramahansa Yogananda

Relationships are similar to jobs in that they involve work but also allow us time to reap the rewards of our work through vacations or retirement. Relationships generally have *work* or *maintenance* phases, wherein we spend time getting to know each other, working through disagreements, and deepening the relationship, *and* then a *vacation* or *relaxation* phase, wherein we should now know each other *well enough* to experience an ease and playfulness with each other. By the time we reach the second phase, we should know what each of us likes and dislikes, thus allowing us to enjoy the relationship to the fullest. By now, we know how to *work* on the relationship when we have to, but we also have earned the right to rest at ease with each other. Any time a relationship lacks ease and enjoyment, it might mean we are stuck in the work phase. This would mean that we either do not know *how* to do the proper work to get us into our vacation phase or that we simply have a "karmic relationship." A karmic relationship is based mostly on unhealthiness and hard lessons and is not about experiencing the vacation phase. If we are in either a "karmic" or a "stuck" relationship, we need to consider getting serious assistance (perhaps with a healer or counselor) or possibly ending the relationship.

The Sufis (and *A Course in Miracles*) teach that there is only *one* of us here. So **everything we experience in a relationship is really just a reflection of lessons and experiences within ourselves**. This is true about the entire *external* world; it is merely a reflection of our *inner* world. **Relationships are the holy altar where we can discover everything we need to know about ourselves through our experiences with others—as we journey home to our Creator, Whom, in Truth, we never left**.

> *He that loves not his brother whom he can see, how can he love God whom he cannot see?*
> —**the Bible** (1 John 4:20)

Relationships often come to bring us opportunities to heal old wounds. But relationships also come as gifts for the healing work we have already accomplished. Again, we will spend much time in our relationships (of any kind) working on the issues that others mirror to us as opportunities for healing. But there also comes a time when we have done enough work and, therefore, have earned love for ourselves. Then we will feel much healthier and more complete, because our relationships will no longer be based on fear and dysfunction, but on love and appreciation. Passion and joy no longer will be experiences for which the ego can demand payment. Our debt now has been paid. We own the relationship: it is ours for healing and for expressing and experiencing love. Now we can take all that we have gained from the growing relationships we have with God and ourselves and share it with others.

Does this mean that everyone around us will be at exactly this same level of relating? Not necessarily! In fact, we can assume that the rest of the world is not yet comfortable with the concept of healthy, fulfilling relationships. Others (including family, friends, and lovers) may still struggle to understand the difference between how we choose to relate and how the rest of the world relates. They often still might want to tell us *who to love* and *how to love*. However, in our new, healthy state of being, we are in a perpetual state of LOVE. To have a partner or *not* have a partner is all the same, but *not* having a partner holds no desperate energy. We are no longer relating out of neediness, but from a place of wholeness. There is no longer dysfunction driven by codependence, and there is no longer codependence driven by erroneous beliefs about ourselves. There is only a focus on sharing our healthy wholeness that keeps growing on a consistent basis. **We each eventually learn to share our True Self with whomever we feel will benefit from the experience, and we will take responsibility for what we gain or what limits we impose.** This level of taking personal responsibility dissolves unhealthy codependence and provides each person with an opportunity to create safe, fulfilling relationships.

CHAPTER TWO

The Three Relationships

There are actually only three relationships we can experience: One is with God, one is with Self, and one is with
Others—including things.

It cannot be over-emphasized that the priority of our relationships needs to be in the following order: first God, then Self, then
Others. This order of priority is crucial because **we would never
be able to express or experience true, authentic love for ourselves or others without having nurtured a reasonable level of
relationship with the Source of Love—God**. Furthermore, we
cannot experience a fulfilling relationship with *others* without having a fulfilling relationship with *ourselves*. This is not to imply that
each of these three relationships needs to be brought to a state of
"perfection" *before* progressing to the next. Instead, all three relationships are generally being developed simultaneously. However,
our relationships *do* need to be given this order of *priority*. This order of priority is empowering and creates healthy interdependence;
any *other* order is disempowering and creates unhealthy codependence.

If, for example, we follow the healthy order of relationships (first
God, then Self, then Others) we will feel a healthy, spiritual connection to *God* in the form of inner peace and inspiration. The fruit of
this spiritual connection will then flow down into our souls and fill

us with a sense of love and self-worth. And, as we continue to develop this relationship with *self*, we will practice a maintenance program of responsible self-healing, while setting healthy boundaries within ourselves. Then, all of these aforementioned attributes (spiritual connectedness, self-worth, self-awareness, and healthy boundaries) will become the foundation upon which we enter our relationships with *others*, and practice clear communication and loving affection.

When we choose to change the order of relationships, for example by reversing the above-explained order, **we end up feeling *disconnected* from Spirit and our inner self. This reversal results in the inevitable search for personal fulfillment *in* others (which is really a search for God and our True Self), rather than bringing the healthy relationship that has been nurtured with God and self *to* others.** This could be referred to as, "looking for love in all the wrong places." Unfortunately, most human beings choose this latter, unhealthy order of relationships. The very idea and misguided notions behind this outward searching for love can only lead to failure.

These are the words of Spirit . . . I know your deeds, your hard work and your perseverance. I know that you do not tolerate egotistic behaviors, nor do you tolerate those who claim to be healthy and spiritual but are not. You have persevered and have honored your Inner Voice. Yet there is one issue to confront: You have forsaken your first Love. Change your course and return to your first Priority—God. Whoever has ears, let them hear what Spirit says to the soul. To the one who gets their relationship priorities straight, I will give the right to eat from the Tree of Life, which is the Tree of Remembrance and the Tree of Enlightenment.

–**the Bible** (Rephrased from Revelation 2: 1-7)

Our first relationship, our relationship with *God*, is primarily nurtured in two ways: prayer and meditation. In a word, these can be summarized as "communion."

Our second relationship, our relationship with *Self*, is primarily nurtured in two ways: healing of self and creating healthy boundaries. In a word, these can be summarized as "responsibility."

Our third relationship, our relationship with *Others*, is primarily nurtured in two ways: healthy communication and authentic acts of affection. In a word, these can be summarized as "connection."

Besides the two ways of nurturing each of these three relationships (with God, Self, and Others), each of the forms of relationship rests upon the criteria *from*, or nurturance *of*, the previous relationship. For example, in addition to our relationship with others relying on the healthy development of communication and affection, our relationship with others *also* is contingent upon all the elements in the first two forms of relationship—our relationships with God and self.

In summary, a person who is having a fulfilling life, through fulfilling relationships, is a person who lives a life of the following: 1) communes with *God*, 2) is responsible with *Self*, and 3) connects well with *Others*.

CHAPTER THREE

The Three Stages
of Relationships

All relationships go through three stages. It doesn't matter what kind of relationship (partner, friend, car, etc.), they all go through three stages—with the second stage having a few of its own options. The following are the three stages: 1) the honeymoon, 2) the honeymoon is over (wherein we usually either go numb and remain in the relationship OR part ways, and 3) choosing to grow and heal—whether the relationship remains intact or not. The latter option, in stage three, is clearly the healthiest option but the option that people tend to choose the least.

Another way we can describe the stages are as follows: 1) romantic love or infatuation; 2) sobering up or falling out of love, which often leads to running out to find someone or something new to re-create the euphoria of the first stage of relationship; and 3) choosing to heal and discover unconditional love—even if we choose *not* to remain in the current relationship.

We can just as easily go through these three stages with a job as we can with a partnership. For example, we might find ourselves in the first stage when we are excited to find a new job. But, inevitably, we will reach the second stage wherein we no longer are looking forward to going to work, or we find ourselves numb and just getting by. We will remain in this second stage until something shifts, which usually means losing the job (just as we do with people) and starting again at stage one with yet another job, which again eventually will end up in stage two. The only way to break this cycle of never finding fulfillment in our jobs is to progress to the third stage of the relationship. This results from having the courage to look at ourselves, heal whatever it is that continually attracts us to unfulfilling jobs, and learn to gain the spiritual connection that will take us from that job and into our "soul's purpose."

Three Stages of Relationships

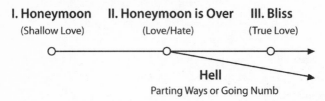

I. Honeymoon
(Shallow Love)

II. Honeymoon is Over
(Love/Hate)

III. Bliss
(True Love)

Hell
Parting Ways or Going Numb

Even when we make it to the third stage of a relationship (whether with a job or a person), the cycle continues, in that we still will find ourselves occasionally challenged by certain aspects of our job, partnership, and so forth. But as we learn to have healthy relationships with God, Self, and Others, we learn how to handle the challenges more responsibly and, therefore, will move through the stages more quickly. In fact, just being aware that these stages exist can make a significant difference in our ability to get through them with more grace and confidence. But such cycles are a *must* because they are a part of life's refinement process. As we go through such cycles in our relationships, we grow and know for sure that there is progress in our ability to share deeper, more authentic, levels of love.

Concerning the relationship between two people, it is entirely possible that two people can actually meet and already share authentic feelings of love and connection. In order to validate the authenticity of their feelings, however, these two people will need to successfully move from the first stage of their relationship through the second stage and on to the third stage. Essentially, **if we feel love in the first stage, this love will be tried by fire in the second stage and transformed into a more authentic love that we find waiting for us in the third stage.** Usually, the more romantic or passionate the first stage of a relationship *seems* to be, the greater the likelihood of a "cover-up" of inauthentic feelings or weaknesses within the relationship. Although we are certainly capable of expressing authentic feelings of love and passion in the first stage of a relationship, there is no "proof" of the authenticity of our feelings until we test them in the second stage of the relationship.

In fact, it can accurately be said that **the ability to make it (or not make it) through all three stages of a relationship (and not bail or go numb in the second stage) reveals just how authentic the relationship was in the first place.** This is one reason why the second stage of a relationship can be so difficult; it is showing us any and all weaknesses we were avoiding in the first stage. So the harder the second stage seems to be, the more we were probably in denial during the first stage. After all, the higher we climb (into denial), the harder we fall. But, whether we know it or not, we all go through these same three stages of relationship over and over. Our goal through this process is to learn to choose more and more often the unconditional love that can be found in the third stage.

THE FIRST STAGE OF RELATIONSHIPS

In the first stage of a relationship, we are usually seeing what we *want* and *need* the other person to be, more so than seeing the real person, with their many layers, who stands before us. And even though the attraction might be strong, the attraction is usually due to our strong need to meet or avoid our unhealed wounds. So, all too often, during those amazing moments when we are falling "head over heels" for someone, we are actually experiencing the set-up for the next stage, wherein we will soon be living-out some of our unhealed wounds.

The unconscious purpose for people who fall in love is to help each other finish childhood. To get the love they want, partners in a relationship must bring this unconscious purpose into awareness, and mutually commit to giving each other the nurturing and validation they did not receive from their parents.

–Dr. Harville Hendrix

When it comes to romantic relationships, the first stage of a relationship is typical, human love with everything looking good and going well. We think a great deal about the other person. They seem to make us feel better inside and out. Most of our time is spent on positive, agreeable interactions: pleasant conversations, making love, nice dinners, and so forth.

The euphoria of the first stage distracts us enough to keep us from noticing what is really taking place. It is quite common for people who end up recognizing the unhealthiness of a relationship to say that they had "no idea who the other person really was." That is because the distractions in this first phase easily prevent us

from noticing the similarities between the people from our past and the people standing before us in the present.

> *A good relationship is one that can survive the ninety-day euphoria of romantic love.*
> **–Edward Abbey**

Rarely do we hear about someone who is experiencing a relationship that resides in the "present moment" with love as the focus—without expectations of filling voids or playing out old patterns. Instead, all too often, relationships are past-based or future-driven.

One of the values of allowing ourselves to be drawn into a relationship based on such shallow premises, as is found in the first stage, is that it allows us to potentially create a bond strong enough to endure the next stage of the relationship, wherein the weak of heart usually go numb or "abandon ship."

THE SECOND STAGE OF RELATIONSHIPS

Now that we have built some history and common interests in a relationship, we may have increased our ability to walk through an occasional crisis or some of the changes that arise *in* our relationship. If we fail to see this, however, it is likely that we will fall into the usual trap of shaming and blaming and end up running away from the relationship prematurely, missing a healing opportunity. **Oftentimes, the discomfort of the second stage results in our seeking to find someone or something new to re-create the first stage of "love."** This level of "love" is far more primitive, shallow, hormonal, and psychological than we may realize.

Enduring the shift from the first to the second stage of the relationship means the spell is broken, and we now will begin to see

deeper (potentially flawed or wounded) parts of ourselves and our partner. This can be a terrifying experience unless we are willing to discover who we are and who our partner really is—beyond our fantasy of what we wanted our partner to be.

In the first stage of a relationship, all too often, people are wearing masks. These masks can appear as false confidence, success, emotional availability, sexiness, and so on. It is not unlike seeing people at a nightclub, wherein they feel that they have to look or be a certain way: strutting, laughing, and flaunting. But, the second stage of a relationship is like the end of the night when the lights come up, and we see everyone a little more clearly, and often, it's not a pretty sight.

In this first stage, **we not only are assigning a role we want others to play but we also are willing to play the roles they assign to us.** We probably will adapt to their false, idealized versions of us just to be liked. In the long run, how can this possibly go well? The truth is, maintaining these facades will not work forever. Unconsciously, we may begin to resent the other person for trying to keep us in that role—partly because it affirms to us that they would not like the real person we are inside. In a sense, this situation is simply replicating our desire as children to be loved and accepted by our parents or friends, but it ultimately represents our beliefs that we are spiritually and personally flawed.

In the second stage, however, things begin to change: the make-up worn in the nightclub comes off, and we begin to see each other's flaws. Here we discover that the other person didn't buy us that drink just because they wanted to be a "giving" person. Instead, they bought us that drink because they wanted something from us. If we were to take that person home to live with us for a while, it is inevitable that we would start to see some of their negative agendas,

traits, and habits. **The more we need the fantasy of the other person to remain intact, the more we will unconsciously (and eventually consciously) begin to resent that person or feel the pain of losing the person we needed them to be.** Of course we will act shocked, but on some level we knew all along that something was not quite right.

> *When you enter a relationship, you feel excitement, enthusiasm, and the willingness to explore. But you may not really understand yourself or the other person very well yet. When you fell in love, you constructed a beautiful image that you projected onto your partner, and now you are a little shocked as your illusion disappears and you discover reality. Unless you know how to practice mindfulness together, looking deeply into yourself and your partner, you may find it difficult to sustain your love through this period.*
>
> –Thich Nhat Hanh

In the second stage of relationship, "the honeymoon is over." The ego now calls for retribution for the illusions that it had encouraged us to embrace. It calls for payment for our momentary bliss. It is as though the ego had only rented us the seemingly "good time" and now wants full payment. Of course, we often have no idea what is actually going on! We have been too busy gazing into each other's eyes, or we may have been too intimidated by a gradually surfacing sense of discomfort.

In this stage of relationship **we often discover that the very thing that we once *liked* about a person becomes the thing we most *dislike* about them.** For example, we might have been attracted to someone for their artistic, free-spirited qualities. Yet now

we are turned off by the fact that their happy-go-lucky attitude has turned into irresponsibility. Another example might be that we once were attracted to someone's "edgy" lifestyle and the unique forms of sensuality that we could share with them. Yet now, in the second stage of relationship, we find ourselves irritated by the fact that their lifestyle might not make them a good parent to our children. We might even consider them less likely to be a *faithful* partner.

When the relationship descends, and the fault-finding begins, it helps to recognize what is happening. We should then ask ourselves if the thing we find annoying is larger than our love and respect for the person. This simple question can assist us in assessing the condition of the relationship. Sometimes this question, followed by its answer, helps us recognize that there is, or isn't, enough love left in the relationship to salvage it.

If we allow the issues that begin to arise to take priority over the choice for mature, authentic love, then we will know that we were not bringing as much unconditional love to the relationship as we had thought. Instead, we were either working on issues from our past relationships or building false hope for a future relationship. Both of these motives keep us from trusting and expressing our True Self in the present. If authentic love is truly our goal, then we will usually find the strength and clarity to push ahead and experience the true love found in the third stage of this relationship.

When we find ourselves in the second stage of a relationship, there are a few things that can and must be done to shift the hurt or stagnation. The most important of these can be summarized as "adding a third party." Now, when people feel this calling inside, they sometimes mistakenly interpret it to mean that they should add another *person* to their relationship—either sexually as a "threesome" or through one of the people having an affair. Others interpret this calling as the time and need to have a *child*.

Models of Unhealthy Relationships

The plus sign represents us and the minus sign represents them.

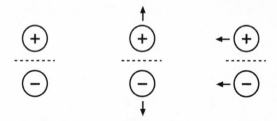

1. No arrows =
No growth

2. Arrows in
opposite
directions =
Moving apart

3. Arrows
moving left =
**Moving
backwards**

4. Arrows moving
from one side
to the other =
Codependence

5. Arrows moving
forward = **Looks ideal
moving forward, but
never getting closer.**

Model of Healthy Relationships

Arrows are going forward
and closer together

+ ⟶ Love
⎯ ⟶

19

In both of these cases, when the intuition or feeling comes that some-one (or some-thing) more is needed, what is happening is that the impulse from the soul to add a third party is mistakenly interpreted to mean that other "people" should be added to the re-lationship. However, this guidance is actually telling us that in order to save the relationship, we need a third party, and the third party in question is not a person but a *thing*.

The "third party" needs to be the *relationship itself*, **wherein we are not merely thinking as "you" and "me" in the relation-ship, but instead, we are also thinking as "we."** What this means is that we need to start thinking beyond our little selves and learn to think as "we"—yet not codependently. Thinking and living as "we" means understanding that every thought, word, and deed in our relationship has an effect on "us." This remains true even when one partner has no conscious awareness of the other partner's thoughts, words, or deeds.

> *So, in each holy relationship, is the ability to communicate,*
> *instead of separate, reborn. Yet a holy relationship . . . is like*
> *a baby now, in its rebirth. Yet, in this infant is your vision re-*
> *turned to you, and it will speak the language both of you can*
> *understand . . . For no two people can unite except through*
> *Christ* [Love], *Whose vision sees them as one . . . This child*
> *will teach you what you do not understand, and make it*
> *plain . . . Yet must He be reborn . . . a tiny newcomer, depen-*
> *dent on the holiness of your relationship, to let Him live.*
>
> —*A Course in Miracles* (T-22.I.7-8)

In other words, **relationships are like bank accounts; the more deposits we make (through healthy communication and ran-**

dom acts of love and affection), **the more we can afford to make withdrawals, which takes place every time we make a mistake** (for example, saying something unkind, being in a bad mood, or doing a hurtful act). Thinking as "we" helps us to set aside our selfishness and pettiness and, instead, make decisions for the greater good of all concerned.

In the second stage of relationships, we are being challenged to grow beyond our previous understanding of who we are and who our partner is. Since we previously had such a strong need to know our partner from a limited perception and to cling addictively to this misperception, it should not come as a surprise that **making these changes in such patterns, for the better, is not unlike going through the same challenges we experience from any other form of addiction**. It is somewhat normal to go through feelings of agitation, anxiousness, impatience, blame, and even panic. The withdrawal-like reactions to the changes in our relationship might also show up in the form of tantrum-like behaviors. We may attempt to control our partner with overt or covert threats and/or intimidation, or we may allow our partner to control us with such behaviors in order to avoid their anger or disapproval. The process is not unlike taking the proper measures to remove a virus from the body; the virus will fight to remain alive and might even attempt to adapt or mutate in order to keep itself alive under the new conditions of the system.

Depending on whether or not we have previously healed and released some of our childhood and family issues, **the second stage of relationship often will evoke our past, unhealed wounds, which typically translates as our partner playing-out some of the characteristics of one (or both) of our parents**. If we "play our cards" right, we will take responsibility, practice good communication, and take the proper measures to heal these former issues now that they once again have surfaced into conscious awareness. If we miss this opportunity for healing by refusing to take responsibility for our feelings and projections, these issues will not disappear. Instead, they simply will resurface in the next convenient (or inconvenient) moment of a future relationship.

THE THIRD STAGE OF RELATIONSHIPS

There is nothing on earth more powerful than the effects of our commitment to reaching the third stage of a relationship. It is here that we discover our True, long forgotten, Selves—as well as the True Selves in others. Such a relationship is even more important than meditation because it becomes the arena wherein we learn to practice whatever we may gain *through* meditation. The possibilities for growth within the relationship are endless, and all parties involved can transcend the "obstacles" (or limited belief-systems) from their pasts and rise to new levels of awareness and experience.

A love relationship requires high degrees of mutual sharing, caring, respect, and involvement. The feeling of being in love is not enough to support a relationship.

–Dr. Howard Halpern

Entering the third stage of a relationship involves raising our priorities, taking responsibility, increasing our self-awareness, being willing to heal our wounds, communicating more clearly, and becoming authentic within the relationship. **The third stage of a relationship involves having a healthier spiritual life and a greater love and respect for ourselves.** With the nurturing of such levels of awareness, we become more evolved. As we evolve, we become better partners and friends, creating safe spaces for those around us.

The third stage of relationship is achieved when we have made it our priority to be a whole being and love as unconditionally as possible. Now Love Divine is our goal with patience and forgiveness as our guide. With such powerful allies, it is nearly impossible to fail! That is, unless we allow our ego to sidetrack us—which it will attempt to do every step along the way.

> *What God has joined together [in the third stage of*
> *relationship], no one can separate.*
> —the **Bible** (Mark 10:9)

In the third stage of a relationship, we are not so much committed to staying in that relationship (job, friendship, etc.) as we are to nurturing fulfilling relationships with God, Self, and Others. Sometimes this is easier to accomplish while staying in the relationship, and other times, it is easier to accomplish by leaving and creating room to breathe.

Fortunately, there are those who have partners who are willing to join them on this quest for wholeness. **With two or more joined in one focus of love, we *increase* the potential of a joyful outcome and *decrease* the amount of work involved.** However, this does not mean that we "need" the other person in a relationship to agree with our chosen goal. This, of course, would not be very unconditional of us. If the other person refuses to walk the path of empowerment and forgiveness with us, so be it. The time will come when they, as we all, will take our issues and lessons with us into another relationship—until we commit to the path of healing and wholeness—as found in the third stage of our relationships.

PART TWO

Our Relationship with God: *Communion*

CHAPTER FOUR

Introduction:
Our Relationship with God

Before we can create fulfilling relationships with *others*, we must first develop a relationship with ourselves (Self) and a relationship with *God*—the Source of True Love. We work simultaneously on each of these relationships, but our relationship with God is the foundation for all other relationships.

> *Turn your attention from this world to the kingdom of God which is within.*
>
> **–Paramahansa Yogananda**

Without the development of our relationship with God, our other relationships are essentially doomed. If (as is often the case in most mainstream counseling), our primary relationship with God is neglected, therapists will continue to have little success in assisting clients in "creating fulfilling relationships." Also, unless authors address our primary relationship with God, they will keep coming up with new theories and models for relationships that continue to lack long-term success. **Without first addressing our relationship with God, approaching relationships is futile.** How can we enhance our ability to love, to be more patient, tolerant, forgiving, trusting, and communicative, without being connected with the True Source of all these attributes—God/Spirit?

Having a "relationship with God" is not to be interpreted as being "religious." Instead, a relationship with God refers to having a relationship with a Higher Power; a Supreme Being; something larger than our small, human, and limited self. It is having a relationship with the creative Source from which All is formed; and, ultimately, it is having a belief in Love in its purest form. This concept of "having a relationship with God" represents profoundly positive feelings: for example, Love, Peace, Joy, Bliss, and Oneness. All such words are synonymous with God and therefore can be used to replace the word "God." In essence, they are all the same: **To become one with Inner Peace, is the same as becoming one with God and to become one with God, is the same as becoming one with Inner Peace.** To feel a sense of Oneness is the same as feeling God. To hold the consciousness of Unconditional Love is the same as holding the Consciousness of God. Such feelings not only lift our heart but also feel quite natural to our heart and soul, when we allow ourselves to breathe them in and live them on a daily basis.

So long as religion is only faith and outward form, and the religious function is not experienced in our own souls, nothing of any importance has happened.

–Carl Jung

To attempt to have a healthy and fulfilling relationship without first having a fundamental relationship with Spirit, at best, may create a life wherein we try to experience love, faithfulness, playfulness, and so forth, but merely at a level of form—without feeling these experiences as an authentic part of us. This form of "fake it till you make it" is dangerous and often fleeting. When we live with our hearts and intention centered in the Spirit of Divine Love, our external love-based behaviors (as well as our internal feelings and inspirations) will be authentic and therefore easier to express and nurture.

Our goal, therefore, is to learn how to access the highest consciousness and feelings possible and then to allow this awareness to guide our every thought or deed—particularly in the context of our relationships. The goal is easy to reach (because, in Truth, it is our natural state) and the benefits are profound.

> *Blessed is he who carries within himself a god,*
> *an ideal, and obeys it.*
>
> –Louis Pasteur

Just as we know a good friend's voice when we hear it, we also can allow God's Loving Voice and Guidance to become very familiar to us, which comes from nurturing a relationship *with* God. To accomplish this, some people spend a lifetime learning advanced forms of meditation and concentration. But there are far easier methods for connecting to the Divine—especially when we understand that we are not separate from God in the first place.

When we connect with feelings such as True Love, Inner Peace, Absolute Bliss, and, Uncontainable Joy, we then feel inspired and uplifted, as well as more in touch with our True Self. Being controlled by our ego, on the other hand, brings us down, deflates and exhausts us.

Hell does indeed exist!—as an extension of our own consciousness. It is a state of mind: it is our conscience, our self-

doubts, the effects of our projections onto others, and the kar-mic effects of gossip and hurtful words and deeds. Also, if there is a devil, it is the part of us that chooses the mindset and behaviors that create this hell.

Love is heaven and fear is hell.
Where you place your attention is where you live.

—Alan Cohen

We can return to Heaven (or remember God) only by choos-ing to give up living in hell through our old, self-sabotaging, ways. We can do this by modifying our mindsets, behaviors, and belief-systems to express love in its true sense with everyone we meet and with whomever we share relationships.

CHAPTER FIVE

Our Divine Father-Mother God

God said, "I AM the Alpha and Omega; the beginning and the end." This means that God is our Source for everything we could ever need—including love. We cultivate this all-encompassing relationship with God by starting and ending our day with remembrance of God through prayer and meditation, or "communion." We integrate our relationship with God into our lives by allowing Spirit to help us make every decision, thus assuring that we remain connected to Spirit throughout the day and yet in a most practical fashion. As we nurture our love for, and trust in, God, we are actually nurturing a more fulfilling relationship with ourselves, which, in turn, assists us in having more fulfilling relationships with others.

Of the three primary relationships (God, Self, and Others) in every person's life, the most important is our relationship with God, or Spirit. In fact, all of our other relationships merely reveal to us the quality of our relationship with God. Indeed, it is virtually impossible that a significant male or female figure in our world does not mirror some aspect of our relationship with God. For example, we often long for approval from our parents in our family of origin, but this merely reveals the deep longing we have for God's approval.

Many of our issues with others (especially our intimate relationships) stem from unhealed issues with our parents. But **our primary issues with others ultimately go back to our lack of fulfilling relationships with God and ourselves**. It should be emphasized, however, that the problem is one-sided and that God is not the one experiencing the problem with the relationship. We are the ones who believe that we separated from the Universal Source of Love and Creation. We then took on the psychological burdens of fear, guilt, and shame for seemingly manifesting this separation. These became the core emotions behind every issue we can experience.

As we grow spiritually and heal psychologically, we retire this propensity to project our unhealed issues onto others. More and more, we allow people to be, or express, who they really are. More and more, **spiritual growth is best measured *not* by what schools we have attended or how many books we have read but *instead* by how little we project onto others**. Projecting less, we are filled with (and perceive) *fewer* of our own projections and *more* of God's accurate and Holy Vision of people, things, and events.

THE DIVINE FATHER

Although God truly has no gender, we can use the concept of "father" to understand the "masculine" aspect of God (or "mother" to understand the "feminine" attributes of God). And we all have three "fathers:" a *Divine* (Heavenly) Father, a *Cosmic* Father, and a *human* father.

We must not confuse the nature of our Divine Father with the imperfections of our human fathers or any other males we encounter on Earth. No matter how good our *human* fathers may have been, their positive qualities never could equal the Strength and Guidance of our *Heavenly* Father.

The Divine Father, who is pure love and inspiration, guides us to new adventures and pursuits. He honors that we *believe* we are on a journey toward perfection, but He *knows* we are already perfect. God's Feminine/Mother aspect takes care of us during our journeys on Earth and comforts us during and after each experience. However, it is the *Father* that calls us to go forth again and complete our lessons until we too have grown (through remembrance) into becoming gods/goddesses.

Although our Divine Mother works with us on a very close basis (like our human mothers cleaning us up after we have been playing all day), the Divine Father seems absent (like our human fathers being at work all day), while making sure all our needs are met. We can easily see the Mother aspect of God in the Earth and all that we draw from the Earth, but the Father aspect is not as easily seen. Like a dad who is at work all day, the Father is not necessarily aware of the details of our days but, instead, knows only the essentials.

Our sometimes flawed *human* fathers might respond (or not respond) to our needs based on their own issues and moods, but not once in the history of humankind has our Divine Father refused to answer the calls of his Holy Children—at least not when they asked from a healthy consciousness. Unlike most human fathers, our Divine Father reminds us constantly that we have already inherited the vast wealth of his Kingdom and should do our spending in His Name.

The first time, however, that our *human* fathers failed to reflect God as perfect safety, perfect abundance, and perfect provision, we became hurt and scared. When we experienced more disappointment, we began to develop a love/hate relationship with our human fathers. Once this occurred and the pattern was set, our human fathers were "doomed" in our eyes, as was anyone we assigned to play out or repeat their patterns.

Through our own projection/perception, this "fall from grace" led to further distancing between us and our other two Fathers: the Cosmic Father and the Divine Father. We now must rekindle a relationship with all aspects of our Father, thus healing the perceived separation and wounds.

The relationship with our Divine Father is renewed through prayer and meditation (or communion with God) and also through nurturing and trusting His Guidance more and more in all aspects of our lives.

THE DIVINE MOTHER

Just as we can use the concept of "father" to understand the "masculine" aspect of God, we can use the concept of "mother" to understand the "feminine" aspect of God: our *Divine* (Heavenly) Mother, our *Earth* Mother, and our *human* mother.

The Divine Mother should not be confused with the imperfections of our human mothers (or any other human females). Again, just as with our human fathers, no matter how good our *human* mothers may have been, they never could have equaled the patience and nurturance of our *Heavenly* Mother.

The Divine Mother is pure love, a love that draws us back to her at the end of each day and after each incarnation. She soothes our wounds and asks us how things went today at the "schoolhouse" of life. She takes care of us, pending the Father's call for us again to go forth and complete our earthly lessons, until we too have grown into gods and goddesses.

When our Divine *Father* created us and we thrust ourselves into the creation of this universe, our Divine *Mother* (in an act of ultimate love) manifested herself as the material universe (matter/mother), like a womb where we could develop. She then helped to birth us into material bodies to complete the incarnation/manifestation process.

Although our sometimes flawed human mothers might respond (or not respond) to our needs based on their own issues and moods, not once in the history of humankind have the Divine and Earth Mothers refused the true requests of our souls, nor has Mother Earth ever refused to give us life or offer us the chemical materials we needed when it was time to incarnate.

The first time our human mothers failed to give us the nurturance we thought we wanted, or needed, we became fearful and suspicious of their love. It is not so much that our mothers failed us; rather, it is that we ended up seeing them as mirroring the lower states of consciousness we were beginning to develop. And, just as we projected this same fear and suspicion onto our human fathers, we secretly began to have a love/hate relationship with our human mothers. Once this had occurred, our human mothers were "doomed" by our negative projections, as was anyone we assigned to play-out this pattern.

Once more, this imagined "fall from grace" of our human mothers led to further distancing between us, our Earth Mother, and the Divine Mother—creating the need for our further healing.

Some people think that getting close to and connecting with the goddess or the Mother archetype manifests as becoming angry and protective of the feminine energy. However, this is far from the truth. Reclaiming our divine feminine begins when we practice such things as nurturing ourselves and others, and when we nurture a healthier relationship with our bodies and the planet on which we live. Care of self and care of planet Earth eventually leads to a healing between us and *all* aspects of the Mother.

THE COSMIC FATHER

If we are in harmony with the Cosmic Father of the vast, multi-dimensional Universe of which we are a part; we know that, in essence, we are one of the stars in His multi-dimensional Universe. We know that, holographically, each synapse in our brain is a star in the universe. Even our physical bodies are composed from the dust of the stars, thus making us a Cosmic "Sun" of God. In harmony with the Cosmic Father, we understand that the gods or goddesses of ancient mythology, immortalized as stars, symbolize who we are and that we are directly connected to all Light-beings of higher, cosmic dimensions. Therefore, we cannot completely know ourselves without knowing the Cosmic Father and vice versa.

We need to remember to remain balanced in our honoring and integration of working with the earthly energies of the Mother *and* cosmic energies of the Father. It is clear, however, that most of us are far more adept at getting in touch with the energies of the Earth Mother than we are with getting in touch with the energies of the Cosmic Father. Being in touch with the Cosmic Father and Earth Mother is similar to being in touch with the yang and yin energies of nature, and both energies are meant to be balanced.

The ancients understood this need for balance between opposites, manifested in masculine and feminine or cosmic and earthly energies. In fact, this balance was not even seen as a "need" but, instead, was maintained just because it was right to do so, as though there were no other option. The Druids, Mayans, Taoists, Lemurians, and others all knew how to walk in balance between the heavens and the Earth.

Today, we can demonstrate and nurture our connection to the Earth Mother by taking time to eat right, go for walks, work-out, do yoga, and so forth. To demonstrate and nurture our connection to the Cosmic Father, however, is accomplished by doing breath-work (such as chi-kung), attuning ourselves to the Star Elders, and studying the influence of the stars and planets. The honoring of the Cosmic Father and Earth Mother are essential ingredients to our living a balanced life and to our awakening. To neglect one or both of these means we are cut off from essential parts of ourselves—living inauthentic, incomplete lives.

THE EARTH MOTHER

Since everything is inner connected, we can draw an analogy between our bodies and the body of Mother Earth. Our physical bodies are her mineral kingdom. Our etheric bodies and energy systems are her plant kingdom. Our emotional bodies are her animal kingdom.

Being in harmony with the Earth Mother (and therefore our own human bodies, our emotions, and our energy systems) manifests as knowing that our breath is her wind; our bones are her rocks; our blood and lymphatic systems are her rivers; our meridians are her gridlines. Therefore, it is impossible to completely know ourselves without knowing the Earth Mother and vice versa.

We need to expand our present limited understanding of the Earth Mother. For example, when we try to protect the Earth Mother from atrocities committed against her, we do her more harm than good if we do so with anger because our anger adds to the Earth Mother's pain by increasing the negativity (hate) in our collective human consciousness.

But when you want money for people with minds that hate, all I can tell is, brother, you'll have to wait.

–Lennon/McCartney (Song: "Revolution")

Someone recently told me of the birth of a white buffalo, which to Native people is always symbolic of hope and new beginnings. Sadly, someone broke into the place where the white buffalo was kept and skinned it alive. The next day they came to also kill the mother buffalo.

As humans, we react to such things with pain and/or disgust, but as souls we are always asked to look within for the deeper significance of any and all events. We need not pray for the white buffalo or the Earth, nor take up arms to fight those who seem to harm her. The buffalo and the Earth are symbols for ourselves and our own hopes and possibilities for miracles. When we destroy them, we are trying to destroy all forms of hope *within* ourselves.

Of course, in the "big picture," there is only God—only Light and Love. In the world we created that overlays God's world (like a veil)—there is fear, ego, and therefore the attempt to destroy Light. As we heal ourselves and planet Earth, we strengthen and heal our relationships with the Earth Mother.

THE HUMAN FATHER

Technically, the human father is in us all. Since the Divine Father offers inspiration and guidance, then it stands to reason that any time we have guided or inspired a new creation for ourselves or others, we have been, or acted as, a creator/father.

If we are called to honor our human fathers, we should *not* do so in a gratuitous or obligatory way. We can, instead, choose to honor only the *honorable aspects* of our human fathers. Jesus never suggested that we get caught-up in feeling indebted to someone just because they are "blood relatives." Instead, he said, "Those who do the will of God are my mothers and brothers and sisters." He also said, "That which is flesh is flesh and that which is Spirit is Spirit."

We have a far greater calling than merely being conditioned by genetics and customs. Furthermore, we really honor our human fathers by being honorable children of all three fathers: Divine, Cosmic, and human.

Honoring our human fathers does not mean enabling unhealthy behaviors, whether ours or theirs. After we reach adulthood, the "parent-child" roles can be dropped. Then we are simply two adults on the path, and sometimes the "child" knows better than, or at least has something to offer, the "parent." After all, adults are not perfect just because they are older than others—especially given that adults merely may have honed their ability to deny their issues, rather than facing and healing them. Furthermore, a man does not achieve the title of "father" just because he has impregnated a woman. The title, in its truest sense, must be earned.

To *ignore* hurtfulness is a false sense of honoring, as is *fighting* the hurtfulness. To find balance is to find peace. If we have peace, we will neither be drawn to the hurtfulness nor will we desire to fight against it. We will only desire to bring peace to this and all things.

THE HUMAN MOTHER

In the final analysis, the Human Mother is all of us. If we ever created a single thing (and we all have), then we all have given birth.

As with our human fathers, if we are called to honor our human mothers, we can choose to honor only the *honorable* aspects of our human mothers. If our human mothers fell into one of the possible polarities of unhealthy parenting (being too absent or overly smothering), it would behoove us to learn what we can from this and to make different choices in our own lives. Despite the successes and failures of our human mothers, if we really want to honor them, then we should practice being honorable children of all three mothers: Divine, Earth, and human.

Being in touch with all three mothers allows us to be in touch with the divine feminine within ourselves. It matters not if we are men or women; we all have attributes of both male and female. Many of us, however, embody attributes of the unhealthy version of either male and/or female. It is, nevertheless, our destiny to eventually embody a healthy version of both the divine male and the divine female. The ultimate goal, however, is to allow the divine masculine and feminine within ourselves to merge: to no longer be discernible as masculine or feminine but, instead, to blend into the Oneness of Pure Spirit.

CHAPTER SIX

Prayer:
Having a God Day

Prayer and meditation are not so much about techniques and rituals as they are about sincerity and humility, or learning to allow God to live through us—as us. Therefore **our prayers and meditations are most effective when they are focused on communing with Spirit and asking to be a clear channel for God's Presence** on Earth—from morning till night and from night till morning.

When we pray, it is best to forget everything about ourselves. We only need to know that we are holding, in our consciousness, the intent to summon an awareness of Divine Presence and then to *become* that Presence. Rather than pleading to an "Entity in the sky" to give us what we perceive ourselves to be missing, we are far better off asking for the assistance from God (Who is always with us) in healing our misperception that we are lacking anything. This misperception is resolved through prayer: by breathing in and simultaneously imagining that the very Presence we used to pray to, is now the Presence that we are becoming. With this awareness, all of our needs are filled, mainly because we now realize we always had whatever we thought we needed. The only real issue is that we forgot who and what we truly are, which resulted in our believing that we are incomplete and in need of many "things."

Seek first the Kingdom of God [the Consciousness of
God] and all will be added unto you.

—**the Bible** (Matthew 6:33)

Our prayers can evolve to the point of experiencing God as our dearest loved One, who rushes to us in time of need and knows our every thought and feeling 24 hours a day. This ever-present relationship with God is the Divine Romance we hear about in many Sufi poems, as well as in the Wisdom Books of the Bible.

The following is a suggested guideline for "having a God day." This simple formula allows us to start and end the day in spiritual consciousness and also reminds us how to maintain this consciousness throughout the day.

START THE DAY

We can start the day with God by "waking up on the right side of the bed." What we do and think in the first seconds of the morning, when we are still half asleep, can have a major impact on the remainder of the day. During these first few seconds of the morning, we are residing between the spiritual and material worlds. Therefore, it is advantageous for us to remain as still as possible, soak in the spiritual vibrations of the higher realms, and take them with us into the material world of our daily experiences.

Because our lower selves are so impressionable at this moment upon awakening (as well as during the minutes before falling asleep at night), it is crucial to be mindful of what we are thinking, feeling, and doing. Instead of allowing the mind to immediately focus on concerns related to the upcoming day, it is more advisable to say a short affirmation or to quietly voice a heartfelt prayer to be of service throughout the day. An example might be, "God, what would you have me do today? Where would you have me go and what would you have me say…and to whom?" Then wait in silence (patiently and without attachment) for a sound, a feeling, a Voice, or even an inspiration.

Starting the day with any thoughts focused on a higher, or spiritual, intention will have immeasurable effects on how we experience the day. Lacking this initial spiritual focus on our relationship with God, our ego-selves quickly gain control of the day by gaining control of our minds and our thoughts.

THROUGHOUT THE DAY

Throughout the day, be sure to reconnect with God. Some guidelines for when to do so, are 1) any random time you remember to do so, 2) during times of transition between one location and another or from one part of the day to another, and 3) on an "as needed" basis. Reconnecting with God throughout the day is the surest way to keep the ego-self from asserting itself. Instead, it encourages the greatest soul growth and allows Spirit to Guide our days.

END THE DAY

End the day with God. Just as it is crucial to start and maintain the day with God, it is also important to end the day with God. For each key event of the day, review the situations that involved someone else. Remember what happened and imagine how that person may have experienced you. In other words, what impact or effect did you have on that individual?

Edgar Cayce indicated that sleep is akin to death; in other words, during sleep (as in death), the soul reviews and digests the lessons of the day (similar to reviewing the life) just completed. Consequently, if sleep really is a preview of the after-death state, then it makes sense to suppose that a process similar to dying happens on a smaller scale each night: There is a review and an attempt to comprehend what has happened during the previous day.

At the end of the day, once you are relaxed and comfortably in bed, go back over each key event of the day. Review and relive the situation as you experienced it. Try to notice your thoughts and feelings—and especially, your motives and purposes.

START THE DAY

1. Invoke an inspirational thought/affirmation.
2. Focus on a mantra (a word or two that are synonymous with God—such as *Love*, *Peace*, and *Joy*).
3. Visualize the coming day flowing smoothly and with many miracles—or shifts of awareness in harmony with God and your mantra.

THROUGHOUT THE DAY

1. Re-focus occasionally on your 1 or 2 word mantra (even if only for a few deep breaths).
2. Re-focus on your mantra whenever needed (even if only for a few deep breaths).
3. Re-focus on your mantra during times of transition (even if only for a few deep breaths).

END THE DAY

1. Give thanks for all that occurred during the day that resonated with your chosen mantra.
2. Focus again on your mantra.
3. Rest in God by gently going to sleep with an intention of entering the higher realms of the Spirit World.

CHAPTER SEVEN

Meditation:
Living the Life

Despite the seeming evidence to the contrary, we are not separate from our Creator. And **since we are not separate, then connecting or communing with our Creator should be far easier than most teachers and teachings would indicate**.

Some would have us believe that the more complicated a meditation technique is, the more effective it will be. But, this is simply not true. The truth is, **the technique we use to commune with our Creator should be the one that most resonates with our own heart-center and feels the most effective to us.**

The following is perhaps the simplest and yet most effective exercise to assist us in communing with the Divine. This exercise is similar to what many shaman refer to as "dreaming the world into being." The best time to practice is each morning when we first wake up and each evening before we go to sleep.

1. Begin by choosing a focus word or words that symbolize the God Consciousness you desire, such as Love, Peace, Joy, Abundance, or Wholeness. This word or words (as already mentioned will become your mantra and represent the new state of consciousness you desire for your life.

2. While you inhale deeply, imagine drawing light through the top of your head from the heavens (symbolizing God). On that in-breath, allow this energy to be drawn down into your heart-center, as you simultaneously concentrate on your focus words or mantra. Pause on the inhale to anchor these qualities (through words and feelings) into your heart-center, exhale slowly as you allow the light to spread from your heart-center to every cell in your body, bathing you completely. As you exhale, allow yourself to hear the words "And so it is." Repeat this process approximately one or two dozen times before proceeding to the next step.

Again, as your draw the energy and vibration of your chosen focus words through your head, you are programming your mind with their meaning. When the energy enters your heart, you are programming your heart and soul. Lastly, when you exhale and allow the energy to pass through your body, you are programming the very cells of your body. Just this step alone, allows every aspect of your being to be programmed with a new level of Spiritual Presence.

3. Now spend at least 5-10 minutes visualizing and feeling your life as you imagine it to be with this new state of consciousness. Look at each major aspect of your life, such as health, finances, relationships, and work.

Ask yourself, "Now that I am indeed filled with 'Love and Self-Worth' (or whatever words you have chosen), what can I expect my life look and feel like in each major category?"

Respond by visualizing and feeling the answer in a living form, as though it is already happening—right now.

For example, if you were to see "Love and Self-Worth" in relation to your health, you might visualize and feel yourself exercising in a form that you enjoy, perhaps yoga. See yourself doing the yoga postures and feeling the effects in your body. This might include seeing and feeling your joints being more open and your body less stiff or sore. You will see yourself feeling strong and vibrantly healthy. What does *that* look like? What does *that* feel like?

4. Always close such exercises by *Giving Thanks* in advance that anything you just imagined, while attuned to Spirit and aligned with your highest good, is already being brought into manifestation.

5. Lastly, in addition to the aforementioned steps, it is important that you make sure that from now on, each decision, action, and word that you choose comes from the focus words you used in Step One. This is how our usual silent meditations become "walking meditations." This new state of consciousness is to be the foundation for building a new life of Love, Peace, Joy, and Abundance.

If our words and actions contribute to our long-term peace and happiness, they probably are the "right" decisions for us. If such actions and decisions conflict with our long-term well-being, they are probably *not* the best choices for us.

In order to continue building our new lives and new, healthier selves with healthier boundaries, it helps to surrender our every thought, word, and action to a Power beyond the laws and logic of this world. **If we follow the tangible guidance in our hearts that clearly promotes Unconditional Love, we can rest assured that this guidance is true Inspiration and is synonymous with the Voice of God.**

PART THREE

Our Relationship
with Self:
Responsibility

CHAPTER EIGHT

Introduction:
Our Relationship with Self

We cannot truly love others if we do not first love God **and ourselves.** It's that simple! Every word or action either reflects a bright and expanding love we have for our Creator and ourselves OR a sad and unfortunate lack thereof. For this there is no argument. **We *see* in others what we *feel* within ourselves.** Therefore, the relationship with others is merely *mirroring* the relationship within our souls. Every ounce of love that is present or absent inside is reflected outside as either love *or* a lack of love for others. Therefore, **the best way to develop better relationships with others is by developing a better, healthier relationship with God and with ourselves.**

Who looks outside, dreams; who looks inside, awakens.

–Carl Jung

As previously emphasized, a healthy relationship with ourselves is built on an increasingly healthy relationship with God, maintained through prayer and meditation (communion). Added to this, having a healthy relationship with ourselves is also contingent upon learning to be more responsible. **"Self-responsibility" involves two**

**primary things: a continued commitment toward self-healing
and self-awareness AND establishing and honoring healthy
boundaries within ourselves.**

Self-Healing, therefore, represents the movement of oneself
(one's focus) from outside to inside. Boundaries, on the other hand,
are the movement from a healthy center inside (discovered through
self-healing) to the outside, wherein such boundaries (or limits) are
then applied—to the outside world.

For many people, the idea of taking responsibility has a negative
connotation, as it is often interpreted to mean "taking the blame."
This is a far cry from the true essence of the meaning. Ultimately,
taking responsibility means to "know thyself." When we know *ourselves*, we truly know who we are: we know a lot about ourselves
and what makes us tick. Not only do we then know our likes and
dislikes, we also know "why" we do whatever it is we do.

> *He who knows others is wise. He who knows*
> *himself is enlightened.*
>
> –Taoist Saying

**To have such an intimate awareness of ourselves means we
have invested time to look within ourselves and to discover
most, if not all, of our major wounds and patterns, as well
as our gifts.** Therefore, we know the roots of our actions and responses, which leads to healthy "response-ability," or our "ability to
respond" in a healthy way.

CHAPTER NINE

Self Awareness:
Know Thyself

If we really want to know what we think about God or ourselves (our inner world), we can do so merely by observing
how we feel about the people and events in our lives (our outer
world). Again, our *outer* world is merely an accurate reflection, or
mirror, of what we think and believe in our *inner* world—inside
our souls. We attract the kind of people and events that best reflect
or reinforce our beliefs, whether these beliefs are held consciously
or unconsciously.

Since most other people have the same beliefs that we are separate from God and each other, as well as having similar patterns of
wounding and woundedness, it is unlikely that they are capable of
giving us all that we believe we "need" from them. It is, therefore,
far wiser to invest our time in getting to know ourselves, healing
our wounds, and dismantling our misperceptions about ourselves.
This, then, eliminates most of the hopeless agendas that we once
assigned to others—namely trying to fill our perceived needs.

Self-healing is one of the essential ingredients for having a
healthy relationship with ourselves, but self-healing is not possible
without the willingness to get to know all intimate details about
ourselves. The internal parts of us that we are not willing to witness

and/or share with others reveal the limits to how deeply we are willing to go on our soul's journey. This is why it so often has been said that the journey of the soul is a journey of courage. **When we hide anything from ourselves or others, it means we are more attached to our darkness than we are willing to discover and share our light**.

Your task is not to seek for love, but merely to seek and find all the barriers within yourself that you have built against it.
    −A Course in Miracles (T-16.IV.6:1)

Knowing ourselves allows us to work towards being a healthier and more whole person. As we come to know ourselves and know what makes us "tick," we become more *responsible* people. **As responsible people, we become *better* people, creating safer spaces in which to share healthier relationships**.

One of the best ways to get to know ourselves is through the practice of self-observation. This is what Edgar Cayce meant when he said, "Stand back and watch yourself go by." He was encouraging the art of self-observation. Practicing responsibility and self-observation are not foreign concepts to anyone familiar with the 12-Step Program. One of the steps in this very effective program focuses exclusively on getting to know one's self by doing a self-inventory.

Without self-observation, we stand little chance of recognizing and correcting our patterns and unhealthy behaviors. **Our egos tend to run our lives, holding us hostage to the programmed behaviors of our woundedness and feelings of low self-worth**. Ironically, most of us are not strangers to the general idea of observation, but we spend far more time observing and criticizing *others* than we do observing and healing ourselves.

That which we do not confront in ourselves
we will meet as fate.

–Carl Jung

Developing our skills at self-observation is made far easier by practicing such exercises as 1) noticing what evokes our most dramatic reactions; 2) observing our inner dialogues—especially with our "inner critic;" or 3) noticing which of our behaviors seem to be automatic reactions, as opposed to authentic responses.

Another way to get to know ourselves is to ask ourselves some of the following key questions:

• What is my greatest fear?
• What is my greatest regret?
• What is my greatest hope?
• What is my greatest talent?
• What is my greatest achievement?
• When do I feel happiest?
• When do I feel most loved?
• How do I respond when my feelings get hurt?

Again, it is important to know ourselves, which includes knowing our deepest feelings. **Not recognizing what we are truly feeling is one of the most common causes of our slipping into judgment**. Once we allow our "inner critic" to pass judgment on us (or others), we are no longer objective. And, contrary to what we want, we energetically become a part of the very thing we are judging and on which we are focusing. Standing back and observing our internal world, automatically allows us to be clearer and more objective in our perceptions.

Getting to know ourselves does not involve only our negative thoughts and emotions; we also need to examine and understand our likes and pleasures. **Getting to know ourselves also involves** *loving* **ourselves—unconditionally.** Unconditional love for ourselves includes treating ourselves with patience and compassion.

Whatever we value most, or are invested in or focused on, is what feeds our souls and thus is what we become. This principle not only refers to the things we value materially but also to our thoughts and imaginings.

> *Where your treasure is, there will your heart be also.*
> **–the Bible** (Matthew 6:21)

The ancient Egyptians believed that when we died, our next destination was determined by the weight of our heart. The heart was weighed on a scale against the weight of a feather. If the heart was lighter than a feather, then heaven was the soul's next destination because it meant the heart was filled with light and lightness—related to having love and care for God, Self, and Others. However, if the heart was heavier than the feather, it meant the person's heart was too weighted down, or burdened, with judgment or sadness—related to God, Self, or Others. The person was therefore sent back to Earth to try again.

Loving ourselves involves choosing to release self-judgment and, instead, allowing our minds to think only what we can think with God, or love-based, peaceful thoughts. In other words, we choose to have only good thoughts—God thoughts.

Our inner critics are similar to the Pharisees and Sadducees of the old world, who often listened to their lower minds, rather than their hearts, when making their decisions—judgments. This is why their words and actions (although following the letter of the law) often expressed hate and jealousy. For this reason, Jesus said that the Pharisees and Sadducees could not understand his message. He told them that their hearts were closed, meaning that they were no longer living in the Garden of Eden (the heart) but, instead, had eaten from the Tree of Judgment and fault-finding, creating the illusion of separation from God/Love.

Loving ourselves also includes maintaining a program of self-healing, having healthy boundaries, and choosing healthy relationships. Loving ourselves at the physical, or material, level involves physical self-nurturance and self-care, as well as being committed toward loving actions. It also includes learning to navigate the waters of our own emotions and thoughts. The potential for our wounds and perceived inadequacies to "pull our strings" lies at the core of all our actions and reactions. These unhealed or unmanaged wounds are at the root of all addictions and, if not addressed, will ultimately undermine our relationships with others.

> *When you learn to get along with yourself, you will know how to get along with everybody.*
> **–Paramahansa Yogananda**

Discovering and uprooting all such unhealthy patterns allows us to replace them with expressions of love and respect for ourselves. This self-love and self-respect eventually becomes abundant enough to where our "cup runneth over," and the love and respect we have for ourselves pours onto, and blesses, the other people in our lives.

CHAPTER TEN

Self Healing

The word most synonymous with having a relationship with ourselves is "responsibility." And one of the primary components of living a life of responsibility involves initiating and maintaining a progressive and effective path of "self-healing." **Self-healing requires a shift in our focus, as it involves embarking on the journey from the outer world to the inner world and from our heads to our hearts**.

Most people take actions and make decisions that seem compelled from, they know not where. Most people do not know the *real* reasons why they choose a particular school, job, or partnership. Many people do not know why they are Republicans or Democrats, nor do they really know why they are meat eaters or vegetarians. This means that **most people go through life, making decisions, small and large, while having little or no idea as to the motivation or cause for their decisions**.

Most people do not know why they are attracted (or repulsed) by certain individuals. Of course they *think* they know why, but that's the problem: they just *think* they know. Not many of us would hire employees or bookkeepers if we were told that they consistently acted out of ignorance, merely *thinking* that they know what they are doing. And yet, without realizing it, **we make so many of our own decisions out of ignorance, for example, not know-**

ing why we feel compelled to pursue certain people. Such unaware actions can be dangerous and lead us to unhealthy decisions and relationships.

In general, most of us just assume that we like certain foods because of the taste and that we like certain people because of their looks or personality traits. But there is far more going on in such attractions than meets the eye. We are attracted to people for numerous reasons that have little or nothing to do with spiritual or authentic connection. The following are some of the reasons why we are attracted to other people:

- Body chemistry (including hormones)
- Karmic connections
- Sexual attraction
- Unresolved parental issues
- Unresolved issues from former partners
- Physical attractions (looks)
- Addiction issues
- Resemblance to someone else
- Primal instincts

We never, then, love a person, but only qualities.
–Blaise Pascal

Self-healing includes the concept of self-awareness, and self-awareness includes the concept of asking ourselves questions to figure out *why* we feel what we feel and *why* we feel what we do for a particular person. Answering such questions gives us the option to override any decisions that are mere compulsions from our lower selves, rather than inspirations from our higher selves. **Asking the right questions, thus getting to know ourselves, also assists** us in accessing answers from the voice of our soul, which can reveal the roots to our actions and decisions.

The soul will then reveal to us one of two general answers. It will teach and reveal to us that all of our motivations come from either the Voice of God *or* the voice of our egos. That's it! There are no other guides or motivators. Although there are various expressions of both God and the ego, there are really only two guides. One Guide leads us with love and inspiration, *teaching* us to find love and inspiration. The other guide leads us with fear and hopelessness, *teaching* us to find fear and hopelessness.

When we choose to embark on the path of self-healing, we are basically choosing to heal and release all of our ties to the ego and all of the wounds that would keep us bound to the patterns that have developed in our lives as a result of choosing our ego as our guide. As we free ourselves from our former ego-based patterns and experiences, we usually develop healthier boundaries, which results in freeing ourselves from unhealthy people, choices, and relationships. We then replace all forms of previous, unhealthy patterns with a new life, guided by God. This leads us to creating a healthier life within ourselves that is reflected outside in the life we are living.

SELF-HEALING EXERCISE: TRACKING

"Self-healing" can be a broad term. For our purposes here, **"self-healing" includes any technique that takes us deeper within ourselves to uncover the roots of our primary core patterns and behaviors**.

Tracking is an incredibly direct, yet powerful and effective, way to access the deeper wounds and/or patterns behind nearly any issue, problem, illness, or crisis. Tracking also can be used to uncover and understand why we make all the choices we make (for better or for worse), which is a valuable part of self-awareness. Anyone can learn to do tracking in a matter of minutes, and the results can enhance the effects of any other form of healing or counseling.

When we are ready to heal ourselves and our relationships, it is essential that we take more responsibility and learn to "track down" the reasons why we seem to be attracted to some people, while others seem to push our buttons. Such responses create what we perceive to be "positive" or "negative" relationships—basically with the people we *like* and people we *don't like*, respectively. However, most of us fail to recognize the real reasons *why* we like or don't like someone. The bottom line is that generally the **people we *like* and think of as "positive" relationships are merely those who bring up *positive* emotions for us. This means, of course, that the people we *don't* like are merely those who bring up *negative* emotions**. So imagine for a moment what it would be like if people refrained from saying "I like that person" or "I don't like that person," and, instead, were responsible and self-aware enough to say, "That person reflects some of the positive gifts in me that I tend to ignore" or "That person reflects some of my negative, unhealed stuff." What a different world we would experience!

As part of our willingness to know ourselves and to discover the roots behind our choices, attractions, addictions, etc., we can use the following tracking exercise (for people, things or events that we are either attracted to or triggered by):

TRACKING EXERCISE
For people who trigger you

1. **Recognize:** Think of a person (or event) in your life that seems to trigger you and begin the exercise by saying (in your own

words), "I recognize that I seem to be bothered, upset, or angered by (insert name) _____."

2. **Accept**: Repeat (aloud or to yourself): "I accept that hidden behind this person are also a few negative feelings such as (name a few emotions—e.g., resentment, shame, feeling controlled, etc.) _____." Then take a moment to see if you can identify any other people or events from your past that brought up similar emotions in you. If so, you are now seeing a "negative" pattern that has resurfaced in your current person. Note that if you had healed this issue in the *past* to the point of completion, it most likely would not be resurfacing in the *present*. This is why we often say that we never really are seeing our current relations in the "present moment," but only from a past, unhealed perspective.

3. **Surrender**: Make a sincere effort to surrender the past experience with this person or event (as well as all the negative emotions around them) to God to be given a clearer, healthier perspective and to be blessed and transformed into a Holy Relationship.

4. **Refill**: Now take 2-3 minutes to imagine drawing Light down from the ethers, through your head, and into your heart for the next several inhalations. At the same time, hear the words, *Love* and *Healing* or *Peace* and *Joy*, or whatever two words you prefer (commonly referred to as a mantra). Then, on the exhalation, simply spread the energy throughout your body as you hear the words, "And so it is."

5. **Give Thanks**: Lastly, prayerfully give thanks to God for the healing, as well as thanking whoever popped up in your exercise, since they now have given you the opportunity to recog-

nize an unhealed memory and an unhealed pattern that you once pushed away and onto someone else. Also give thanks that you now have chosen to fill yourself with a greater abundance of God.

TRACKING EXERCISE
For people to whom you feel attracted

1. **Recognize:** Think of a person in your life whom you seem to like or are attracted to (which can also be a food, alcohol, or anything material) and begin the exercise by saying (in your own words), "I recognize that I seem to be drawn toward, or attracted to, (insert name of person or thing) _____."

2. **Accept:** Repeat (aloud or to yourself): "I accept that hidden behind this person (or thing) are also a few positive feelings such as (name a few emotions—e.g., stimulated, excited, attractive, appreciated, happy, etc.) _____."
   Then take a moment to see if you can identify any other people, events, or memories from your past that brought up similar emotions in you. If so, you are now seeing a "positive" pattern that has resurfaced in your current person (or thing). Note that if you had integrated this person or events in the *past* to the point of allowing yourself to own (as your own talent) this good characteristic, or trait, it most likely would not be resurfacing in the *present*. This is why we were told in the Ten Commandments to not "covet our neighbor's goods." What this meant (in part) was that instead of seeing something we value in someone else, we should absorb it and own it for ourselves.

3. **Surrender:** Make a sincere effort to surrender to God the past choice to believe that these positive traits were not within you, but, instead, were seen only in someone or something else. Af-

ter prayerfully choosing to own and affirm them for yourself, surrender the past event or relationship to God to be blessed and transformed into a Holy Relationship.

4. **Refill**: Now take 2-3 minutes to imagine drawing Light down from the ethers, through your head, and into your heart for the next several inhalations. At the same time, hear the words, *Love* and *Healing* or *Peace* and *Joy*, or whatever two words you prefer (which is commonly referred to as a mantra). Then, on the exhalation, simply spread the energy throughout your body as you hear the words, "And so it is."

5. **Give Thanks**: Lastly, prayerfully give thanks to God for the healing, as well as thanking whoever popped up in your exercise, since they now have given you the opportunity to recognize a pattern wherein you had rejected your own goodness and transferred it onto someone else. Also give thanks that you now have chosen to fill yourself with a greater abundance of God.

CHAPTER ELEVEN

Boundaries:
Our Spiritual Muscles

M ost people might assume that the topic of boundaries would be covered when discussing our "relationship with others." Instead, we find it here, when discussing our "relationship with self." The reason is that boundaries begin within *us*. **Boundaries might often be applied *with* others, but they must *originate* within *us*.**

The single most important thing to remember about boundaries is that **healthy boundaries are never determined or decided by others but are always determined by *us*** and our connection to Spirit, for they are rooted in the core of our being.

Often people think that having weak boundaries is a sign that we are *weak* in our relationships with *others*. The truth is, a lack of healthy boundaries *originates* in a weak connection to *God* and ourselves and then is merely *reflected* in our relationships with others. As we heal our connection to God and become more responsible with ourselves, our boundaries with others not only will be stronger, but also easier, and more natural.

When we fail to set healthy boundaries, it is a sure sign that we are feeling disconnected from Spirit and from our inner self. With this personal sense of disconnection, we begin to experience an unconscious desperation stemming from our internal sense of emptiness. This desperation leads to our increasing tendency to make rash decisions or decisions that might seem to somehow fill our emptiness, but always fails.

One of the most obvious examples of this desperation is seen in the "rebound relationship." **People who enter a relationship when they are "on the rebound" know on some level that such a relationship is probably not a good idea. Nevertheless, their desperate need to feel loved or their fear of being alone often overrides common sense and healthy boundaries.** In such instances, if people would "check-in," they could search their souls and find a voice that advises them to take time to heal any unresolved issues from previous relationships before they enter a new relationship.

Year after year, individuals all around the world work to develop healthier boundaries. All too often, they find that the progress is slow or sometimes completely unsuccessful. The primary reason for this lack of success is *ignorance*. **Most people do not know what boundaries are, much less how to set them**.

The origin of boundary issues is generally the same for everyone and tends to digress along the following lines: We forget who we really are; we feel empty inside (on a deep unconscious level); we go about our lives either taking from others, to feel more complete, or we constantly give, in order to feel more complete. Such bargaining, referred to as "codependence," actually is rooted in the collapse of our boundaries.

> *To accept your littleness is arrogant, because it means that you*
> *believe your evaluation of yourself is truer than God's.*
>
> *−A Course in Miracles* (T-9.VIII.10:9)

Boundaries help us to become more responsible. In fact, one of the most mature and responsible ways of expressing love is to set healthy boundaries *on* our self and *with* others. **When we set healthy boundaries *with* others, we are actually demonstrating more love and self-worth *toward* ourselves, which in turn, allows us to be more loving *toward* others.**

Healthy boundaries are *not* meant to be walls, barriers or defenses. To set boundaries does not mean learning to say "no" more often. Actually, it is less about saying "yes" or "no" and more about knowing *why* we are saying "yes" or "no." **Establishing healthy boundaries is based upon knowing who we are *spiritually* and knowing what we can afford *personally* (financially, psychically, emotionally, etc.) in any situation.**

Boundaries are much like the human aura; they emanate from within our being and form a protective shield around us. If our auras and/or boundaries are weak or tattered, then we become more susceptible to the harmful influences of people or of toxins in our environment. Also, like our auras, boundaries are not walls, or barriers, but are intended to be flexible and to adapt to circumstances that may vary from day-to-day. The safer we feel, the more expansive our auras and boundaries can be. But the more unsafe we feel, the more our auras and boundaries will respond by constricting in an attempt to keep us safe.

Boundaries mark the point where our energy ends and another person's begins. The problem within dysfunctional or codependent relationships, however, is that **the weaknesses in one person's boundaries (and energy-field) send a message out to other more dominating people (who have their own boundary issues), letting them know that there is someone out there whom they could dominate to seemingly raise their ego-based self-worth.**

Most people assume that if people lack healthy boundaries, they tend to be "victims" in the world. In truth, however, **a lack of healthy boundaries can take the form of either a controlling victimizer *or* a controlled victim**. Both parties are equally broken inside, and therefore they both lack healthy boundaries. Some people with victim patterns allow themselves to seem weak and susceptible to being controlled. They often look like victims and are often the recipients of the hurtful deeds of the victimizers— who *appear* to be strong but also still have weak boundaries. The behaviors in either example *appear* to be opposites and tend to feed our propensity for judgment when we think we see victims and victimizers, or "good guys" and "bad guys." In truth, however, both types of people (victims and victimizers) are basically the same. They lack a connection to Spirit, as well as a connection to themselves. This lack of connectedness makes them feel insecure. Then, as a reaction to feeling insecure, one person crumbles, seemingly defenseless, and the other steps in and takes control. But the core insecurity in each is exactly the same. They just cope with the feeling of disconnectedness and insecurity in different ways.

Healthy boundaries reflect the *healthiness* of each person, and a *lack* of boundaries, therefore, reflects the *unhealthiness* of each person—physically, emotionally, mentally, and spiritually. If we are healthy *inside* (mentally/emotionally/spiritually), this healthiness will be reflected in our *outer* boundaries. Thus, internal and external healthiness (good boundaries) allow us to feel safer, clearer, and more confident to engage in healthy relationships.

Boundaries can manifest at various levels and in various forms. For example, we all have *physical* boundaries, such as our personal possessions, our personal space, and our bodies. We all have *mental* and *emotional* boundaries, such as energy, personal information, interests, personal needs, thoughts and ideas, feelings, and choices. We also have *spiritual* boundaries, such as our choice of religion, spiritual practices, and spiritual beliefs.

There are several ways to know for certain if we *lack* healthy boundaries, but the most common symptoms of a lack of boundaries are as follows:

Intimacy issues—not having healthy boundaries creates all kinds of problems related to intimacy, including the tendency to push others away or the opposite tendency to overly cling to others.

Giving more than receiving—a lack of mutuality and respect in relationships.

Betrayal—the people around us gossip about us or they fail to keep our personal information confidential.

Lacking confidence—needing to depend on others to help us make our decisions, even decisions about what we feel and/or what we believe. Also going along with the thoughts or opinions of others, rather than honoring our own thoughts and opinions.

Lacking a personal force field—which tends to make us vulnerable to taking on other people's energy, moods, and emotions.

Feeling too much for others—which means getting caught in other people's problems.

Feeling empty inside—resulting in our attempting to fill the emptiness with the presence of other people.

Being overly sensitive—taking to heart what others think or say about us.

Having anger or rage issues—which usually come from feeling too vulnerable, exposed, or hurt, but not knowing how to process such feelings in a healthy way.

Feeling false or fleeting happiness—happy feelings based only on things in the outside world.

Frequent disorientation—having a hard time knowing how we really feel.

Toxic relationships—choosing unhealthy or even dangerous partners and/or remaining in such relationships too long.

Lacking self-care—not having alone-time and/or not taking care of our health, nor receiving enough healing or pampering.

Negative emotions—feeling excessively anxious, shameful, afraid, or unsafe in our environments.

Being taken advantage of—people taking things from us without asking or borrowing money or possessions from us but not repaying us or returning the items.

Being too naïve—trusting in untrustworthy people who end up hurting us.

People invading our space—too often having people push themselves on us or take over our space.

Failing to stand up for ourselves—not knowing when or how to say "yes" or "no" at the right moments.

Not having our needs met—possibly not even knowing what our needs *are*, let alone knowing how to get them *met*.

The best way to know for certain that we have healthy boundaries is by checking-in on how we *feel*. If we feel a sense of inner peace, clarity, and connectedness, we can probably rest assured that all is well with our boundaries. We can also use the state of our *external* relationships to reflect to us how we are doing *internally* with our boundaries.

There are several ways to work on, repair, and strengthen our boundaries, thus making them an expression of healthiness. These would include doing and experiencing the opposite of the above symptoms of having *unhealthy* boundaries. Other methods for creating healthy boundaries include the following:

- Healing old wounds (through counseling, various healing arts, a 12-Step Program, etc.).
- Taking better care of ourselves (physically, emotionally, mentally, and spiritually).
- Dealing with our own emotional issues that make us suseptable to weak boundaries and codependence (for example, self-doubt, low self-esteem, unhealed wounds, and fear of abandonment).
- Nurturing a healthier psychological and spiritual life.

When we do not feel safe or when we are being harmed in any way, our boundaries usually have collapsed or are collapsing. When this happens, we often regress into becoming the wounded "inner child," not thinking clearly enough to negotiate our own safety. Obviously, **if we regress to being like wounded children, we will not have the faculties or experience to know how to deal with the dramas and dangers of the world.** This is an unfortunate form of what is often called, "age regression," since children have no idea of how to be protectors or healthy parents. The only solution, therefore, is for us to develop a healthy relationship with Spirit and with our own healthy selves—allowing the frightened child within to be brought to these healthy parts of us for protection and healthy parenting.

Following this healthier course is the opposite of age regression and can be referred to as "time convergence" because, instead of the child being dragged into the patterns and wounds of the past, time is collapsed; and the frightened child is brought into the present, safe moment. Ironically, **if other people trigger us into experiencing age regression, they themselves usually are feeling their own form of age regression.** It often fails to look like that because *their* age regression may demonstrate a false sense of strength, when in fact, they merely turn into a bully, throwing a tantrum and trying to harm others.

Whenever we feel frightened, intimidated, or even out of control, the best thing to do is to take some deep breaths and recognize what is really happening. Something is pulling us out of our center and possibly causing us to retreat into the fight, flight, or freeze response. Once we recognize this, it helps for us to seek a safer place as soon as possible—finding a safer and quieter *external* environment, as well as a prayerful or meditative *internal* environment.

People not only are conditioned to have weak boundaries as children, but from feelings of low self-worth and a lifetime of negative patterning, they also learn how to bargain away their boundaries as adults. For example, we sometimes go out with someone just so we are not home alone. We take jobs that are not part of our soul's purpose just so we can pay the rent. Or, we share intimacy with someone just so they will like us or so that they will not be angry if we say "no." All of these are acts of bargaining away our boundaries.

As we heal, we learn that **if people in our lives do not *add* to our sense of love and self-worth, then they more likely, *take away* from it.** Therefore, when creating fulfilling relationships with others, we are learning to honor our inner selves and our boundaries. We soon realize that by being true to our spiritual Self, we are rewarded with relationships that are authentic and end up adding to (not taking away from) who we truly are.

SETTING & HONORING BOUNDARIES

Although it is great to care for other people, we also need to love and care for ourselves by not giving to others when it means sacrificing our own center of being. Consequently, **setting healthy boundaries should become a normal part of making our day-to-day decisions**—large or small. For example, if someone asks us to spend the day helping them with household chores and we know we have only a few hours available, setting and honoring healthy boundaries might take the form of our agreeing to help, but *only* for the few hours that we know we are available. So, rather than attempting to set boundaries by saying emphatically, "I am not helping you with that . . . I do not have time," a healthy person, with clearer boundaries, might say instead, "I would like to help you out but, considering my schedule, I do not see any possible way. But here are my available days and hours. So if I can be of any assistance during these times, please let me know."

When you allow others to over-persuade you, or when you rely too much upon others, there is not the use of the innate strength within self. But let your yeas be yeas and your nays be nays— though [centered] in the Lord . . . knowing deep within yourself you are right [to honor yourself]!

–Edgar Cayce

Healthy boundaries might take the form of saying "no" but without the usual feelings of guilt. And no matter how good we get at setting boundaries, it is something we will continue to do for the rest of our lives, as a natural part of our developing relationship with ourselves and with others.

Boundaries are like our spiritual muscles that help us enforce what we believe to be our higher good. Therefore boundaries must be exercised by learning to honor what we believe to be true in our hearts: sticking to our decisions, but remaining flexible; tactfully and confidently stating our needs; and developing healthier discernment.

Setting boundaries is not unlike practicing a passive form of martial arts, wherein people who are trying to harm themselves or others sometimes have to be restrained. Doing so can give them a moment to calm down and possibly shift somewhat from their egos' influence. And, although setting boundaries with others should rarely, if ever, involve force or harm; if this does become necessary, such actions should be taken without anger or judgment. Of course **as people become more responsible and have healthier boundaries, they do not require others to set boundaries with them**.

Setting boundaries with others is like saying NO to an *addiction*. The part of us that is addicted (the ego) may not like it, but it is for the greater good of everyone involved. In fact, the ego is never happy or satisfied, which means that most people will not appreciate anyone putting limits on their egos' behaviors. But this need not be our concern. Our intention is to love others, but this means loving the real (Soul) part of them and not the unreal (ego) part. And, setting limits on the unhealthy behaviors of others will aid and encourage them to find their true essence in a healthy relationship with themselves. So **its okay to walk away from others when their egos scream too loudly, as this action of healthy-minded boundaries might make them try harder to say "no" to their own egos**.

A good example of setting healthy boundaries is found in an old story of a cobra that was terrorizing an Indian village. This cobra was causing much fear amongst the people. One day a visiting master came to the village and heard about the problem, so he went to see the cobra. He asked the cobra why he was terrorizing everyone, and cobra explained that it gave him great pleasure. When he heard this, the master patiently and compassionately explained to the cobra that the greatest pleasure came from being loving and kind, not from bullying others. The cobra listened and with deep humility promised to change his ways. The swami left on a journey and several months later returned to the same village. At the edge of the village, he encountered the same cobra, now bruised, battered and covered in dust and grime. The master immediately asked what happened to cause his pitiful condition. The cobra explained that once the villagers understood that he was no longer threatening, they turned on him and beat him up. The swami sighed and with great compassion said, "But I never told you not to hiss!"

If we fail to set boundaries when people are being hurtful, we are actually enabling their unhealthy behavior. When we set healthy boundaries, it is like placing a limit on our unhealthy choices and behaviors or on the unhealthy choices and behaviors of others. When we *do* choose to draw a line and say "no" to a behavior, it is best to not come from a place of judgment of ourselves or others. On the contrary, we might be saying "no" to an unhealthy behavior, while feeling love and compassion. For example, **we might choose to set a boundary to end a relationship,** *and* **choose to continue loving the person.** However, we do not have to move in with that person or continue with the relationship on a daily, intimate basis.

Setting boundaries is not the same as trying to "control" others or make them behave in a way that "suits us." It's more like saying, "Here is what works for me." But we have to be careful that we are not consciously or unconsciously trying to control others, as this would mean that we do not accept them as they are. **Setting healthy boundaries means that we should not settle for or accept the behaviors of others when they are obviously being hurtful.** We are encouraged to know *what* works for us and what does *not* work for us and to then stick to our boundaries in a loving, but firm, manner. If others perceive our boundaries as an attempt to control them, we have the option of tactfully explaining that their behavior might actually be fine for them or for others, but not for us. We might even encourage them to choose friends or partners with whom this particular behavior is agreeable.

Setting boundaries does not mean we are judging ourselves or others as somehow being bad or hopeless. Their purpose is to support a life of peace and wholeness and with the greatest good for all. **When we set and honor healthy boundaries, we are merely setting limits on how much "drama" we will allow, or on how "out of divinity" we will allow ourselves or others to go.**

This does not mean that boundaries are tools that "good" people apply against "bad" people. **Boundaries are set and honored so that all people can become healthier.** Ultimately, in Truth, we are all one, and "others" are reflections of our inner self. Therefore, when we set and honor healthy boundaries, we are setting limits to what we will allow our own egos to project onto what we perceive as "others." We are choosing instead to honor our Higher Self, thus choosing to create a life that reflects more of God and less of the ego.

Many who are on the spiritual path often ask if setting boundaries isn't confirming that we are failing to love the other person "unconditionally." However, unconditional love and boundaries are not mutually exclusive. Unconditional love is a feeling, while boundaries are an action—albeit an action determined by our being centered in Divine feelings (such as Love, Peace, Joy, etc…). **Our job is to maintain love and respect for the souls of all people, while simultaneously making decisions that keep everyone's actions in alignment with that love and respect.**

> *Let others do as they may, but for me,*
> *I will serve and honor the way of God.*
>
> –the Bible (Joshua 24:15)

One of the times we most need to set boundaries with others is if/when we are in a "no-win situation," such as when someone tries to engage us in an argument wherein no matter what we say, it seems to be the wrong thing. In such a case, setting boundaries might take the form of excusing ourselves from the argument or insisting that the tone of the conversation change for the better. Our setting of boundaries also is clearly needed when there is no apparent progress in a conversation or in a relationship.

An easy and practical way to set and apply boundaries with someone who has been selfish or hurtful and wants to "make things right" is to simply allow them to "repent," which in modern terms (and 12-step programs) means to "apologize and make amends." To "apologize" means that they offer a heartfelt apology and are willing to do whatever it takes to clean the slate, improve the situation, and clear the karma. Making amends allows people to clear their souls and is a good practice for everyone who has acted selfishly or hurtfully.

In conclusion, it becomes appropriate, healthy, and necessary to set boundaries against the ego-based behaviors of other people—meaning to put some limits on what we will allow their egos to act out. However, we need not *hate* them, nor do we need to feel "better" than they are. Our action of choosing right-minded boundaries might very well help to create the shift in their awareness to look within and begin their own self-healing process.

PART FOUR

Our Relationship
with Others:
Connection

CHAPTER TWELVE

Introduction:
Our Relationship with Others

Healthy relationships with others can be summarized in a single word: "connection." All of our challenges and issues with *others* ultimately stem from our belief that there *are* "others" and that we are somehow separate and disconnected from them. This belief results in the tendency to feel threatened by, or in competition with, others. The solution to this "madness" is to learn to create a healthy, safe sense of connection with others. Furthermore, **if we remember that we are all one, we will have no problem communicating with and appreciating one another, sharing acts of kindness and affection, and sharing true love.**

When you meet anyone, remember it is a holy encounter. As you see him you will see yourself. As you treat him you will treat yourself. As you think of him you will think of yourself. Never forget this, for in him you will find yourself or lose yourself.

—A Course in Miracles (T-8.III.4:1-5 & 5:12)

Again, we can have three relationships: God, Self, and Others. Each of these relationships is nurtured in its own way. The last relationship in this list, **the relationship with *others*, is nurtured** through keeping the first two relationships intact (the relationships with God and self) and then adding healthy *communication* and *connection* (affection and healthy intimacy) with others.

The first two relationships are absolutely essential to having fulfilling relationships with others, because we cannot possibly have fulfilling relationships with *others* if we do not have healthy relationships with *God* and *self*. Without healthy relationships with God and self, we will be walking the world feeling empty, desperate, and needy.

> *There are lovers content with longing.*
> *I'm not one of them.*
>
> –Rumi

So to *have* healthy, fulfilling relationships with others, we have to learn to *bring* healthy relationships (with God and self) *to* others. In other words, most of us go *to* others to *get* a relationship *from* them when we actually need to learn to share *with* others the relationship we *already* have with God and Self. **We enter into relationship not to *get* anything, nor to *give* anything, but rather to *share* unconditionally that which we already *have* and what we already *are*.**

Since the three relationships (with God, Self, and Others) are so interconnected—and ultimately are One—the more we nurture and experience deep, authentic, fulfilling relationships, the happier we will be. Conversely, if our lives lack deep, authentic, fulfilling relationships, the unhappier we will be. We most likely will spend much of our lives either numbing the pain of this unhappiness or choosing, time and again, people or things that *seem* to satisfy us initially but inevitably fail to fill our inner void. In fact, at the root of all forms of addiction on Earth (whether sedation or stimulation) is this attempt to numb our pain, or falsely fulfill ourselves.

Because we hold a core belief that we are separate from God and from each other, we entered this Earth realm already having issues to heal. Then we entered our families of origin carrying issues of separation, as well as unresolved issues from previous lifetimes. So **our families of origin are not the first cause of our issues and patterns but, in the present lifetime, they *are* the first effect**. Although it is appropriate to do healing work around our issues with our families of origin, it is not appropriate to assume that they are the root cause of our issues, nor the only manifestations. **Our families were chosen to exacerbate or magnify the issues held deeply within our souls**, in order for us to become aware of these core issues and work to heal them.

> *Relationships [with others] are our opportunity*
> *to see ourselves in every way imaginable.*
> **–Gregg Braden**

Another source of unhealed issues and patterns may come from anyone we attempted to use in order to compensate for what we failed to receive from our families of origin, which includes our childhood friends and eventually our boyfriends, girlfriends, bosses, and early partners. These individuals, like our families of origin, are not the initial causes of our core issues; rather, they are the effects (the mirroring of our already established issues). Whatever traumas or issues we experience in such relationships will add new levels of wounding—unless, of course, we experienced loving, expansive, and fulfilling relationships with these individuals.

The purpose of a committed, intimate love relationship is to . .
. foster the development of the undeveloped, originally projected
aspects of both [people's] personalities.

–Don Lathrop, M.D.

One thing is certain, though, no matter what we perceive to be the cause or effect, **all wounds must be brought to healing, and every hurt attached to them, released.** This is done through the process of healing. And make no mistakes about it: healing (and forgiveness) is a process—not an event. Through the process of healing, we learn to give ourselves the love and respect we may not have received from our families of origin, childhood friends, or adult partners.

Once we reach a certain level of healing, we actually reach what could be referred to simply as being "born again," which actually feels like being re-parented, not by family figures on the outside, but by the Source of Love itself—God. Once we begin to experience this re-parenting process, we will recognize and utilize God as our Spiritual Parent; and, in addition, God will utilize us (our True Self) to re-parent some of the parts of our wounded inner child.

In or out of relationship, whatever we feel belongs to (or has its origin in) us. Therefore, in actuality, **other people have little or nothing to do with what we are feeling. They may be the match that lights the fuse, but the powder keg is already sitting inside of us, waiting to be lit.**

Our belief that we are separate from the universal Source of Love is so deep and strong that we see and experience this false belief mirrored in all we do, feel, and experience—in every relationship we encounter. Therefore, ultimately, every relationship and experience is fated to reflect to us either that we are separate and consequently lonely and afraid OR that we are temporarily loved but with a love that will evaporate, leaving us again feeling lonely and afraid. However, this emotionally painful pattern can be broken if we heal the erroneous belief at its source. In other words, because our core belief that we are separate from love is bound to show up as our experience—through our relationships—the feeling of separation from love will continue to be our experience until we change (or heal) our core belief. **Once we change our false belief to the reality that we are not, and have never been, separate from God/Love, our experiences and relationships will begin to reflect this new level of consciousness.**

Remember the best relationship is one in which your love for each other exceeds your need for each other.

–**Anonymous**

When we heal our connection to Spirit and to ourselves, we will be able to share healthy communication and affection with our partner (and, in an appropriate manner, with all people). Then our lives will change forever—for the better. The work to achieve this level of awareness may seem formidable, but it's worth every bit of effort and we will end up healthier than we might ever have imagined possible. We will feel spiritually connected, as well as know ourselves far more intimately and responsibly. Also, we will be closer and more authentic with others. This means that we truly will be living the good life—a fulfilling life with fulfilling relationships. Ultimately, there is nothing else more important than having healthy, fulfilling relationships with God, Self, and Others.

CHAPTER THIRTEEN

Relation-ship Versus Relation-shit

When speaking of relationships with others, there are generally just two kinds of relationships: *karmic-relationships* (relation-shit/cell mates) and *gifting-relationships* (relationships/soul mates). *Karmic relationships* are the relationships that come to us mostly to represent lessons we think we need to learn or healing that we feel we need to accomplish. *Gifting-relationships* are the relationships that are repaying us for the lessons we have *already* learned and the healing we have *already* accomplished (at least to some significant degree). Karmic relation-*shit* is experienced when we still find ourselves stuck with cell mates and "dumping on each other." The gifting relation-ships are experienced when we learn to recognize that we are "in the same *boat*" with soul mates and need to learn to navigate the waters of life together—as *one*, rather than as divided.

"And the two shall be one" is one of the oldest descriptions of a relationship. This often misunderstood quote is frequently thought to mean that when two halves (partners) are combined, they will create one complete person—a good description of codependence. However, this quote is really meant to describe the intention and result of two beings sharing the same commitment to discover their own wholeness—a good description of healthy interdependence.

A symbol of the ideal relationship is that of two circles partly overlapping. This symbol suggests that in order to experience fulfilling relationships, three entities (God, Self, and Others) act as one. When these three entities are seen as one and are experienced as though they have no separate interests, then we feel and see peace and harmony in our lives and relationships.

Three Models of Relationships

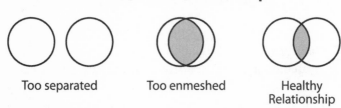

| Too separated | Too enmeshed | Healthy Relationship |

All of our experiences, in or out of relationship, arise from the blueprints of our belief systems. These blueprints exist deep in our souls and are referred to in metaphysical circles as our "Akashic Records" or our record in the "Book of Life." Since these blueprints exist in our souls, then the deepest core of our issues are not *psychological* problems, as much as they are *spiritual* problems. This is why psychotherapy, without a spiritual approach, remains limited to dealing with an emotional effect of our soul-level issues (albeit better than dealing merely with physical symptoms).

A primary aspect of relationships, impacted by our soul-level issues, is that of romantic love, particularly when it comes to "falling in love." There are basically two ways of "falling in love:" Awake—where we fall in love with a *conscious* attempt to truly love more fully; or *Asleep*—where we mostly are *unconscious* and assume we are more fully experiencing love. In either case, there is potentially either a great excitement and/or a great terror. In one regard, we excitedly long to let down some of the barriers we have raised to protect ourselves from the pain of believing that we are separate from Love. On the other hand, we are terrified of the vulnerability that results from this letting down of our walls. Of course, this terror does not help us to create positive outcomes. In fact, this very fear will be the most common reason why we fall *out* of love.

The resolve to merge solely with one other fuels the practice of self-discovery and healing.
–Steven Levine

Often when we experience "being in love" (which can be a microcosm of real love), we are so frightened that we eventually begin to find flaws in our partners or friends in order to justify shifting from trust to distrust. If we were aware and took responsibility for this shift from trust to distrust, we would catch our ego's fears of being too close to a potential healing. However, our unconsciousness keeps us bound to our original, unhealthy contract and pattern, and we allow the illusion of fault-finding to be the justification for our judgments and our eventual reason to run away from the relationship. Of course this running away is just another way to act out or manifest the belief that we are separate from Love and not able to connect effectively with others.

The erroneous belief that we are separate from God, and from each other, leads all human beings to one of the most fundamental core feelings—that of emptiness. **Because we feel empty inside, we search the world for something to fill that emptiness.** The "thing" we find and believe to be a solution to our deep, spiritual and psychological pain may be alcohol, drugs, work, sex, or even other people. Whatever we believe the solution might be, in actuality, will not work. The effect it may *seem* to have is only temporary, leading to more intense feelings of emptiness, which cause us to desire more of whatever we think fills our emptiness (or other forms of it). Rooted in a belief in separation, this pattern is the genesis of all addictions.

Most people are not aware of the core *belief* that we feel separate, but they might be aware of some of the core *issues* that stem from this belief: feelings that we are flawed or that we are lacking or that we are not lovable.

If we fail to see our mistaken core *beliefs* and their birthed core *issues*, they will take the form of core *patterns* in our lives, such as feeling betrayed or abandoned or alone. **Then, if we fail to see our core beliefs, issues, *and* patterns, they will descend one more level into the material world and become our *experiences*.** They actually manifest as the events and people in our lives who most demonstrate to us that we need to take a more honest look at ourselves and our lives. Therefore, it is important to work on healing the roots of these problems and the various forms they have taken in our lives.

When we learn to make the healing path a permanent part of our personal practice, we will spend more time uprooting the false beliefs and patterns about ourselves and replacing them with the truth of who we are as divine beings—made in the perfect image of Love (God). **When we live healthier lives, with clearer understanding of our true Self, we tend to no longer look outside of ourselves for people and things to fill our emptiness.** This step is essential in creating fulfilling relationships.

But if we continue to maintain the false beliefs that we are separate, alone, and empty, we will look harder for a partner and become tenser and more desperate. Then, the tenser and more desperate we become, the more likely we will find tense and desperate partners—even though the form of their tension and desperation may look different from ours.

Emotional relationships are relationships of desire, tainted by coercion and constraint; something is expected from the other person, and that makes him and ourselves unfree.

–Carl Jung

The very act of looking already affirms that we "do not have" and, thus, must "seek to find." Therefore, the outcome cannot be promising. Instead, a better idea is to first have a healthy, loving relationship with God and ourselves, and then allow the healthiness of these relationships to attract other healthy people (not just random partners) into our lives. These people are more and more likely to be emotionally and spiritually healthy. Also, having many new, healthy people in our lives increases the odds of discovering one or more people with whom we resonate and whom we begin allowing into our lives at a more personal level.

As we develop a healthier, more authentic sense of who we are, we are more likely to meet others who mirror this healthiness and authenticity back to us, thus increasing our odds of having more success in our relationships. After all, how can we expect our relationships (in any form) to exceed our own sense of healthiness and self-awareness?

RELATION-SHIP:
HEALTHY/INTERDEPENDENT RELATIONSHIPS

Healthy, fulfilling relationships are grown, or nurtured, not found. Once we find ourselves in the midst of a developing relationship, it is important to give the relationship time to grow—or-ganically, or naturally. It is important to take time to talk, share, and really get to know each other with conversations that are open, honest, and thorough. It is also important to discuss any relevant history, the kind of relationship we want, and even discuss some of our core issues and patterns and how we deal with them, rather than taking them out on others. Of course, we have to know ourselves well enough to be able to share this level of maturity with others.

Love is not a relationship. Love is a state of being; it has nothing to do with anybody else. One is not in love, one is love. And of course when one is love, one is in love—but that is the outcome, a byproduct that is not the source. The source is that one is love.

—Osho

As "issues" begin to arise (and they *will* arise) between us and our new companions, it is a sure test of how much we have (or have not) really grown and how prepared we are for a relation-ship. It might be that we find we can indeed make it through the test (of this second stage of a relationship) OR we might find that this attempt at a relationship was just a "dress rehearsal"—showing us where we need to step back and do more work before the real curtain goes up.

To make it through the tests that arise, it is necessary to prac-tice keeping our center (not losing control and becoming reac-tive), watching our issues and reactions (and healing them as they arise), communicating clearly and responsibly, and offering gifts of love and affection (words and acts of kindness, not objects).

Love endures only when lovers love many things together and not merely each other.

—Walter Lippmann

Besides the development of our spiritual and personal selves, so necessary if a relationship is going to succeed, there are several other ingredients to a healthy relationship that include the following:

Commitment: Commit to being fully present in each relationship. Being present means not allowing our minds or hearts to wander or live in a fantasy of being elsewhere with others. Commitments can be made for one hour or one lifetime. It is important we do our best to commit only for periods of time that we truly believe we can handle, as well as have the integrity and honesty to let all involved parties know if the commitment changes in any way. Lastly, we need to commit to ourselves and honor the priority of our inner, personal health.

Sharing: A fulfilling relationship always includes a great deal of sharing. The average relationship is based on giving and taking, which is all about bargaining. But a fulfilling relationship is based on the sharing of that which we feel we *have* abundantly and can *afford* to extend to others. Some options of what we can share with others include time, connection, dreams, interests, feelings, lifestyles, intimacy, values, and spiritual ideals. It is unlikely that we both will be interested in sharing all of the same things, but the more we do, the greater the chance we will have a fulfilling relationship. However, the areas where we do not share the same things, are the areas that might gradually *grow* into mutual sharing, which might take weeks, months, or even years.

Growth: In a fulfilling relationship, growth is expected and accepted, which includes growth in the relationship and growth individually. Encouraging and enjoying growth in each other is a sign of mutual love and respect. If a relationship lacks growth, it might mean it is experiencing stagnation.

Communication: Healthy and responsible communication is one of the most essential aspects of a fulfilling relationship. Healthy communication involves love, objectivity, respect, clarity, responsibility, trust, and tactful honesty. Since communication involves at least two people, and since we sometimes are more the speaker and other times, more the listener, it behooves us to develop our abilities in both roles of communication.

Responsibility: As we grow spiritually, it is inevitable that we will learn to take more responsibility for ourselves—our own feelings and experiences. Being more responsible, however, includes understanding the law of "mirroring." The law of mirroring tells us that whatever we see or experience in others is a mirror of either something we like or dislike in ourselves. Being responsible also includes being accountable for our choices, and for our actions and reactions, as well as for honoring our boundaries.

Unconditional Love: Love, in its practical application, includes being spiritually mature and having a forgiving heart. Without the practice of forgiveness, there is no love. Being unconditionally loving does not mean always acquiescing to the demands or unhealthy behaviors of others. When we practice unconditional love, we are choosing to not confuse the person/soul with their unhealthy behavior.

When people fail to nurture the above qualities, then it might be time to take a deep breath and ask themselves (and possibly their partners) some crucial questions that may very well determine the fate of their relationship. These questions might include some or all of the following (or other questions of your own choosing):

- *Am I still in love, or is the love I feel merely a memory of the love I once had?* There is a difference.

- *Are my negative feelings a sign that I have fallen out of love or just a sign that I am irritated?* If you are just irritated, ask yourself which of the following is stronger: the love that you have for your partner or the irritation you are feeling?

- *Is it possible that I am frustrated that my partner doesn't want to grow with me?* If so, it is usually more likely that instead of the main issue being that your partner refuses to change, the truth is, although you liked them the way they were when you met them (or else you probably would not have been attracted to them), *you* have changed since that meeting. And even though you may have changed for the better, you are *still*, nevertheless, the one who has introduced a change into the dynamics of the relationship. Therefore, although you may not feel called to remain in the relationship, your partner might deserve some extra patience and compassion while you are still there.

- *Am I willing to make some dramatic changes (such as seeing a couple's counselor) for this relationship?* In other words, do you want to help make the relationship work?

- *Would I recommend my type of relationship to anyone else I love?* For example, if I had a 16 year old daughter, would I confidently support her if she were considering a similar type of relationship?

- *Am I willing to continue this relationship (as is) for another 20 years?* How about 10 years? How about 5 years? Am I willing to continue another 1-2 years?

If you fail to respond with a confident "yes" to any of these, it means that either a dramatic change must be made for the positive or you can expect a change will come that might *not* feel so positive. Either way, the relationship will call for a change—the easy way or the hard way. (In the first of these two options, we can play a part as co-creators; but in the second of these two options, we are more likely to seem powerless and feel like victims.) To help you make the change, ask yourself the following:

- *What option will bring the greatest good, to the most people in the long run?* Some of your decisions will cause short-term disturbances in people's reality but consider the long term effects.

- *Can I honestly say that I have done all I can to make things work in this relationship?* Have you learned all you need to learn from this relationship? If you leave, leave because you have done and learned all you can, NOT because you think there is something better or easier somewhere else.

In the event that you feel guilty or regretful for having to make such a decision, ask yourself if it is your intention to be hurtful to the other person. If this is not your intention, then consider letting yourself off the hook for having to make such a choice.

YIN & YANG IN RELATIONSHIPS

Relationships are generally made up of two people. And, although we can assume that the male partner is the stronger (yang) personality and the female partner is the softer (yin) personality, such is not always the case. In fact, in same-sex relationships there is no guarantee that just because we have a same-sex relationship, we will have two strong or two soft personalities. The truth is, **we can learn more about relationships from the ancient Oriental concept of** yin and yang than we can from gender stereotypes for men and women.

So instead of assuming that men and women each have certain characteristics, that they are fated to remain this way, and that their gender is the determining factor; let's consider this ancient model for the balancing of male/female energies (yin and yang) that remains applicable to this day.

In each relationship, no matter what the gender(s), there is generally going to be one stronger, assertive personality-type and one softer, passive personality-type. And, in the world of Oriental medicine and philosophy, the universe is made up of an interplay between these two forces—yin and yang—that seek balance between one another. Therefore, **when we observe a relationship and are tempted to assume that we are seeing an example of one person dominating another, it is more than likely that the universe actually is attempting to teach each of them to seek balance**.

For example, one of the people involved might be excessively passive and so that person attracts someone who will help them experience an unhealthy and opposite extreme by overcompensating for their passivity. Instead of making the usual observations and judgments about such a relationship and jumping to the conclusion that the passive person is a "victim" and should immediately leave, or be rescued from, a "victimizer," consider that as long as that person continues to be excessively passive, the universe will continue to bring them yet another form (person) of assertiveness to dominate them. This pattern will continue until the excessively passive person finds inner balance between their passive (yin) and assertive (yang) energies and will, therefore, be more likely to attract another person who is similarly balanced between yin and yang energies.

GROWING RELATIONSHIPS

When we observe the speed with which most people enter relationships, it is easy to recognize this common tendency to act in an unhealthy manner and make uninformed decisions. If we move too quickly into a relationship of any kind, we may miss (or be unaware of) the agendas we are bringing into our relationships. There may be such subtle agendas as not wanting to grow old alone, wanting to share financial responsibilities, or wanting to feel more attractive or appreciated. All of these are unhealthy reasons for entering a relationship.

Although it is possible to be instantly attracted to someone (or feel "love at first sight"), who very well may be healthy for us, such a relationship (like all others) needs to grow and develop over time—at a pace wherein we are able to observe ourselves and each other. The relationship should maintain a pace wherein we are able to retain our center, our sanity, and our boundaries. If ever the relationship rises to a speed where we tend to lose ourselves or the time to check in or to communicate, we have entered dangerous territory and need to slow down, possibly even stop. We need to take a step back, so we have space and time to breathe, gain an objective viewpoint, and readjust.

> *Let there be spaces in your togetherness,*
> *And let the winds of the heavens dance between you.*
> *Love one another, but make not a bond of love:*
> *Let it rather be a moving sea*
> *between the shores of your souls.*
> *Fill each other's cup but drink not from one cup.*
> *Give one another of your bread*
> *but eat not from the same loaf.*
> *Sing and dance together and be joyous,*

but let each one of you be alone,
Even as the strings of a lute are alone
though they quiver with the same music.
Give your hearts, but not into each other's keeping.
For only the hand of Life can contain your hearts.
And stand together yet not too near together:
For the pillars of the temple stand apart,
And the oak tree and the cypress grow
not in each other's shadow.

–Kahlil Gibran

THE PYRAMID MODEL OF
THE LEVELS OF RELATIONSHIP

Some people refuse to date unless they know for sure that the person they would date is "the right one!" If we do this, however, it can place an unseen pressure on each person that we meet on our search for a relationship. Also, there's little chance of us enjoying the journey. Not only do we need to "lighten up," but we need to become a healthier version of what we want to find in others; and by so doing, we are more likely to see reflections of goodness in others and to attract healthier relationships.

One of the best ways to practice "growing a relationship" is to avoid the pitfall of having conscious or unconscious agendas for anyone we meet. **All too often, when we meet others, there is an agenda, an agenda that can range from having sex to becoming life-mates**. One method of preventing this pitfall is to use this "Relationship Pyramid." Like all pyramids, this Relationship Pyramid has several blocks on the bottom row and fewer blocks on each consecutive row moving upward until the top, which has one single capstone.

Using the "Relationship Pyramid" analogy, we can see how "unaware" people, have a tendency to rush relationships by immediately trying to make a person into the "person of their dreams," thereby instantly placing that person at the top of the pyramid (as their capstone). However, any person we just met should be, by analogy, merely another person on the bottom row of the pyramid and should not be placed immediately on a higher row—least of all the capstone. In other words, all of the people we meet should be seen as individuals who may or may not progress to the next row of the pyramid.

Relationship Pyramid

A person we choose as a lifemate ————————————————

People with whom we choose partnership ——————————

People with whom we choose to be monogamous ——

People with whom we choose to be intimate ———————

People we choose to date ————————————

People we choose to get to know ————————

People we meet ————————————

The bottom row of the Relationship Pyramid (which obviously has more people than the row above it) represents all of the people we meet at any given time, including acquaintances. The second row represents people we consider getting to know more—developing a friendship. The third row represents people we would consider dating (maybe, maybe not, exclusively). Then, the fourth row (which clearly has a lesser number of people than the previous rows) represents people we might consider inviting into our home—perhaps for dinner or to watch a movie. This row also includes people we might choose as lovers.

Continuing the analogy, the few people who eventually reach the higher rows of the pyramid (which could take anywhere from several months to a few years) are those with whom we clearly have chosen to be in a deeper, more intimate (possibly monogamous) relationship. At this point, we have developed a connection, friendship, and greater intimacy and are ready to commit to a partnership (possibly live-ins) or even a life-mate relationship.

Sometimes the order of the levels of relationships may vary, and there are occasions wherein a stage or two may be skipped (for various reasons). For example, we sometimes become monogamous as soon as we start dating. However, **it is imperative that all parties concerned know the exact level of the relationship**. Otherwise, one person may assume the relationship has reached one level (such as monogamy) but has failed to communicate this to their partner, who is still under a different assumption (such as, that it is still okay to see other people).

Again, as we grow relationships, we go through several levels; however, we should not assume that there is a goal (such as reaching the top level). In fact, **the relationship can be harmed if forced to reach a level that has not been achieved through an organic, or natural, progression**. The time it takes to go through the levels, or stages, of a relationship varies considerably. The healthier we are, the less time it usually takes to develop deep relationships. Such healthy people, however, are not to be confused with people who are so unhealthy that they tend to rush into relationships or rush the progression of the relationship. The crucial factor is the *depth* and *quality* of the people involved, rather than the *speed* with which they go through the stages, or levels, of developing a relationship.

Unfortunately, however, some people meet many other people (who are like the numerous blocks on the bottom of the Relationship Pyramid) and begin having sex with them before these people have moved into higher and more appropriate levels of the pyramid. The message conveyed by such unhealthy behavior is one of desperation and possibly a lack of integrity. The people who would respond to such an unhealthy message are the ones that some of us end up dating and then complaining about days, weeks, or months later. **Some of us often may wonder how it is that another person failed to be the capstone in our Relationship Pyramid when (by analogy) we never built and developed the proper foundation and layers to the pyramid—we never got to truly know and connect with that person on a meaningful level.**

Many a man in love with a dimple makes the mistake of marrying the whole girl.

–Stephen Leacock

The Relationship Pyramid analogy helps us to relax, letting go of the obsession to find the "right one." We can understand that it's important to socialize, meeting other people while seeing them as merely first-level possibilities in a Relationship Pyramid. In other words, **we can refrain from obsessing over thoughts and agendas about where the relationship might go and just** *date* **someone.**

TIME-FRAME AGREEMENTS

When it comes to pacing ourselves in relationships, **we should consider creating a time-frame agreement if (or when) we finally do decide to commit to a relationship.** To some people, this idea may seem ludicrous; but for most people, it is ingenious and effective. Time-frame agreements allow us to pace ourselves in a relationship. Also, they help us to become more present because we tend to feel safer when we create greater clarity for the goals and direction of the relationship. Some couples might choose a six-month agreement for the timespan of their relationship, while others might choose a one-year agreement.

Either way, the points of the agreement should include a commitment to being as present (and engaging) as possible throughout the duration of the agreement. Each person also should agree to share as much openness and trust as possible. At the end of the agreed-upon time-frame, the couple can decide to add another period of time (ranging from a month to several months). If the concept of a time-frame agreement is not acceptable, a good couples' counselor could help a couple to navigate their relationship. However, time-frame agreements have the potential to save us time and grief and can help us to create the best relationships ever.

RELATING WITH OTHERS

The word, "others" has a similar root as the word, "outer." There-fore, it should be remembered that our approach toward relation-ships with others includes our relationship with *anything* outside ourselves—such as *other* people or *outer* objects.

When we project our issues onto others, we do so to avoid looking at what is inside of us. Such projection is possibly the number one weapon in our ego's arsenal meant to prevent us from taking responsibility. This strategy never actually works because whatever it was we tried to avoid by projecting outward, now is front and center in our outer lives in the form of people and life's circumstances—refusing to go away until faced, owned, and healed.

Every person, all the events of your life are there because you have drawn them there. What you choose to do with them is up to you.

–**Richard Bach**

On the other hand, the opposite of projection is "extension"—both of which involve our sending of messages (beliefs) from our inner soul (mind) out into our world. The difference is that **painful thoughts and beliefs become *projections* that take the form of fear-based, uncomfortable experiences, while loving thoughts and beliefs become *extensions* that take the form of loving, comfortable experiences.**

If you begin by sacrificing yourself to those you love, you will end up hating those to whom you have sacrificed yourself.

–**George Bernard Shaw**

It is written that in a town of people who knew him too well, and took him for granted, even Jesus could not perform miracles. Similarly, if we take others (including our partners) for granted, miracles of change are less likely to be witnessed. Instead, our hearts and minds must be open to seeing people and circumstances differently, such as through the eyes of unconditional love and/or forgiveness.

The most important ingredient to a fulfilling relationship is the ability to know how to share love with one another, while remaining responsible for our own issues—rather than projecting them onto each other. This two-fold process is called "responsibility" and "forgiveness."

One of the most under-rated and under-used expressions of forgiveness is the practice of patience, understanding, and tolerance.

Extending gifts of love such as these is one of the most profound ways of helping others to feel loved and accepted—as they are.

So few souls or entities have combined love in the material plane with tolerance! For, love in the material becomes egotistical, and this is opposite from tolerance.

–Edgar Cayce

Practicing tolerance is a good way to cancel out the constant nagging of our "inner critic." Instead of "pouncing on" what we perceive to be the shortcomings of others; if we practice love combined with tolerance, we can choose to allow them to be as they are. Also, we can look at what part within us finds it necessary to notice, or perceive, shortcomings in others.

Tolerance is not to be confused with enabling hurtful behavior, nor is it to be confused with not knowing our boundaries. Being tolerant simply means choosing to love the *good* qualities in another person more than being annoyed by (or fearful of) what we perceive to be the *bad* qualities. Being tolerant and understanding also means choosing to be responsible for looking at (or tracking) our own issues hidden behind our annoyances with others, while keeping an open mind and respecting other people's points of view.

RATE YOUR RELATIONSHIP

The idea of "rating" relationships may sound strange, but that is because many of us are not used to having clarity in our lives. Using the following simple technique for **rating a relationship gives us a clearer picture of the status, or health, of our relationship and its many facets.**

First, write a list of five or ten categories of your relationship. This list should include such things as communication, beliefs, affection, lifestyle, sexuality, and so forth. Next, on a scale from 0—10 (zero being the lowest rating and 10 being the highest rating). Then take a moment to rate the relationship, in general—meaning your overall level of happiness and satisfaction with the relationship. Then rate each category of the relationship individually. When done, you can average the rating of the *individual* categories and see if they come close to your original *overall* rating of the relationship. Either way, when you review the individual categories, you should be able to see what areas of the relationship are the strongest and weakest.

A lot can be learned from this review: One of the most important things is having a clearer picture of which areas of the relationship need the most work. **For some people, rating their relationships can be a very sobering experience and can result in a realization that the relationship might be too far gone**. But for other people, the recognition of which areas are weakest could be life-altering, as they now can get to work on those specific areas, which could save the relationship.

If changes are necessary in order to make it possible to remain in the relationship, then we need to implement those changes—immediately. The longer we take to make those changes, the less likely the relationship will last. However, this exercise is not just about deciding whether or not to end a relationship; it's also about becoming aware of the status, or health, of a relationship. **Possibly the only thing worse than staying in an unhealthy situation longer than necessary, is not even being aware that it is an unhealthy situation**. But by asking direct questions and rating our relationship, we bring clarity and awareness to our situation, and greater awareness always creates the potential for greater change—usually for the better.

KARMIC RELATIONSHIPS
VERSUS GIFTING RELATIONSHIPS

There are generally only two types of relationships: "karmic relationships" and "gifting relationships," and both have their own reasons for creating attraction.

In *karmic relationships*, we are attracted on several primal, human levels (i.e., chemical, psychological, dysfunctional)—all of which lack the deeper inspirations behind *gifting relationships*. If we *are* self-aware, however, these relationships can give us an opportunity to heal dysfunctional relationship issues as they surface.

Gifting relationships, on the other hand, do not come to us primarily for the karmic reasons of working out old issues. Instead, they come to us primarily as *gifts* for the good work we *have* done on ourselves or with past relationships. Gifting relationships in their purest form clearly are rarer than karmic relationships. **In order to know for sure which type of relationship we are encountering, we first need to have a relationship with ourselves.** If we are not self-aware and do not know how to go inside and ask what is happening and why, there is little opportunity for us to enter a relationship with our eyes "wide open."

AFTER THE LOVE IS GONE

If, for any reason, we decide that our relationship (be it with a friend, co-worker, family member or partner) cannot be salvaged, then we might try taking a break from the relationship in whatever form seems most appropriate. If this too fails to create the dramatic shift needed to salvage the relationship, then **sometimes we simply have to part ways—which should be done with as much love and respect as possible.**

There are people in your life who've come and gone.
They let you down; you know they hurt your pride.
You better put it all behind you baby; cuz' life goes on.
You keep carrying that anger, it'll eat you up inside.
I've been trying to get down to the Heart of the Matter.
But my will gets weak, And my thoughts seem to scatter.
But I think it's about forgiveness . . . Forgiveness.

–**Don Henley** (Song: The Heart of the Matter)

Even though our goal may be to heal all of our relationships, **sometimes there is simply too much "water under the bridge" to create an external healing with some relationships.** In order to discover if it is too late to create an external healing, we can ask ourselves if we have done everything possible to create such a healing. We also can ask ourselves, "What would be the greatest good for the most people in the long run?"

Of course, if we were to leave a relationship without doing everything possible (internally and externally) to create a healing with that relationship, the odds are that we will confront the same issues again in a future relationship— even if that future relationship is not a romantic relationship. If we become disillusioned from repeating unfulfilling relationships, we may wonder why we seek (or are attracted to) such relationships. If a relationship comes to an end by our choice or the choice of our partner, **we need to take time to grieve any losses and be vigilant for any lessons we might need to learn and patterns we might need to heal**. Otherwise, we very well may be "fated" to re-create the same type of lessons and patterns in future relationships—even if the names and forms of the people change.

All too often, people assume that if they end a relationship, they have somehow failed themselves or others. Some well-intended people even believe that if they are truly "unconditionally loving," then they should not have to end a relationship. This, of course, is dangerous thinking, as it could override our healthy boundaries by implying that we should allow people to do whatever they want to us and that we are supposed to accept it.

Expressing unconditional love does *not* mean that, no matter what the circumstances, we have to continue a particular relationship. Having unconditional love means that even if we part ways, we will remain committed to refusing to blame or judge the other person. Also, we will continue to affirm the spark of Divine Light within that person, and to love that Divine Light, their True Self.

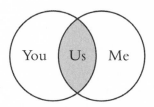

When we view the symbol/model of a healthy relationship (two circles slightly overlapping), we can see that if any relationship comes to an end (for any reason), the individuals themselves remain intact. In other words, although the overlapping of the circles dissolves when the shared relationship ends, you and the other person each survive and only the relationship comes to an end. Now it is up to you and the other person to part ways with as much love as possible and take any remaining lessons with you.

RELATION-SHIT:
UNHEALTHY/CODEPENDENT RELATIONSHIPS

Unhealthy, codependent relationships are usually more for-*getting* than for-*giving*. In an unhealthy relationship, our emptiness calls for a filling up with whatever has been erroneously assumed to be the solution to a seeming lack. So the tendency is to keep wanting, needing, and/or asking for something of our partners. Even when such a person gives, it is usually with an agenda of how the "favor" will later be paid back in the form of meeting their wants or needs. Unlike this unhealthy pattern of giving in order to get, true love is synonymous with unconditional love—which comes with no agendas and, instead, offers itself freely.

Codependency is based upon the false belief that we are *dependent* upon others for our state of being and feelings, whether positive or negative. The genesis of codependence is as follows:

- We believe we are separate from God, which then results in our disconnecting from our own sense of self.
- The perceived separation from God results in our feeling a seemingly unquenchable emptiness.
- Feeling separate, empty, and desperate, our boundaries (and personal energy-field) collapse.

We go out into the world looking for something or someone to fill our perceived emptiness, and of course nothing can succeed at this, mainly because we actually are not separate. However, because of our collapsed boundaries, we are willing to bargain away our higher good to receive any sense of self—however false or temporary it may be.

Since our false attempts at filling ourselves fail, we try again and again, thus turning these attempts into an addiction.

Generally speaking, **codependent people often *appear* as benevolent and giving. The problem however, lies in the conscious or unconscious intention for their giving**. Healthy people give from the inspiration to give, and they give only when/where they can afford to give—not at the risk of their own health and boundaries. A codependent person, however, often gives to others no matter what the costs may be because they lack a healthy sense of self.

Codependence does not always appear in the form of someone who "takes abuse" from a partner. It can also disguise itself as someone who seems to be in any of the following categories (or labels):

- Rescuers and Fixers
- Over Achievers
- Failures (or inadequate)
- Perfectionists
- Falsely Confident
- Selfish or Narcissistic
- People Pleasers
- Victims or Martyrs
- Addicts
- Abusers or Bullies

Codependence usually (but not always) implies the presence of at least two people who tend to be unhealthy in their self-awareness and boundaries. However, it is possible for a single codependent person to attempt to act out unhealthy patterns with others who may not be codependent. The results in such scenarios will vary from one relation to another. **The most obvious signs, however, of a truly codependent relationship is that there is likely to be an obvious victim and a victimizer**—one person who appears to be controlling and the other person who seems to be weaker and more compliant.

Such codependence does not happen overnight. Usually, it is learned by either direct experiences or by what we have witnessed in our early years of development. Codependency, is much like a progressive disease that worsens, rather than improves, unless treated.

Codependents are usually rescuers. A codependent/rescuer is often someone who does one or more of the following:

- Does something for someone that the other person did not ask them to do OR insists on doing more than he/she was asked to do
- Insists on doing something for others that the person prefers to do themselves
- Does something for someone that he/she resents doing
- Helps someone to gain value, or look good, in the eyes of others

Healing codependence or any codependent relationship involves breaking some very deep and often life-long patterns and usually is best accomplished with the assistance of an experienced counselor and/or a 12-step group that focuses on healing codependence. The signs of healing codependence often include the following:

- Gaining a greater sense of our spiritual and personal self
- Developing healthier forms of communication
- Shifting from outer orientation toward inner orientation
- Developing and honoring healthy boundaries
- Healing past wounds and patterns
- Learning to take greater responsibility for self
- Developing a clearer sense of what we feel for others and why
- Seeing an obvious improvement in all relationships
- Feeling more autonomous and free
- Less likely to feel like, or be, a victim
- Feeling an improved amount of personal value

Addictions are rampant and affect every human being in one way or another—directly or indirectly. In every country we find people who are addicted to alcohol, drugs, or sex. And although not *all* people are addicted to sedatives or stimulants (which includes sex), most people *do* suffer from some form of codependence. Therefore, it stands to reason that codependence is the most rampant of all addictions in the world.

Basically, our codependent self is just one of the identities, or masks, that we wear to cover up the ego. When the ego coaxes us to surrender, or lose connection with, our true, divine self, it then replaces our true self with the false, codependent self.

You ask me to enter but then you make me crawl and I can't be holding on to what you've got when all you've got is hurt.

–U-2 (Song: "One")

Healing ourselves of the pattern of codependence is not a one-time event; rather, it is a process, as well as a maintenance program. If we see that the signs of healing (listed above) begin to lessen in our lives or if we begin to notice their opposite (symptoms of unhealthiness) beginning to manifest, then we should take action immediately to turn things around and manifest more healing.

A Course in Miracles (a brilliant manual of spiritual psychotherapy) shares vivid explanations about the unhealthiness (codependence) of nearly every relationship on Earth and how they can be turned into healthy (interdependent) relationships. The "Course" refers to *unhealthy* relationships as "special" relationships and *healthy* (or healed) relationships as "holy" relationships. The *Course* says that special relationships are called such because they are referring to the "special" assignment we give to our codependent relationships—to help us avoid and cover up our wounds.

The term for *healthy* relationships in *A Course in Miracles* is "holy relationships." **"Holy relationships" refer to relationships that have been surrendered to Spirit and have therefore been healed and transformed.** This transformation shifts a relationship (wherein we were either avoiding our issues or projecting blame *for* our issues) into a sacred and holy relationship that has successfully gone through the three stages of relationship—resulting in a state of unconditional love. *A Course in Miracles* describes the characteristics of codependent (special and unhealthy) relationships and interdependent (holy and healthy) relationships to be as follows:

The Special (codependent) Relationship
- Focuses on the needs of the body and the material world
- Only loves conditionally
- Uses relations to avoid inner issues
- Blames others for personal issues
- Makes others responsible for our happiness
- Holds resentments for perceived harms
- Encourages guilt, shame, and inadequacy
- Makes us look for good and bad in others and see it as real

The Holy (interdependent) Relationship
- Focuses on nurturing a relationship with God and the recognition of our divinity
- Loves unconditionally
- Uses relations to heal inner issues
- Takes responsibility for personal issues
- Takes responsibility for our own happiness
- Practices forgiveness
- Encourages peace, joy, and self-worth
- Allows us to see the holiness in others

CHAPTER FOURTEEN

Communication

M ost partners claim to know each other fairly well. But **one
of the most tragic things about relationships is that few
of us in a partnership know our partners' greatest dreams and
fears.** We might know our partners' favorite colors, foods, TV shows,
or even sports teams. However, almost no one knows what lies in
the depths of our partners' souls—our partners' greatest dreams and
fears. If we do not know these dreams and fears, it might very well
mean that we really do not know our partner's heart and soul. How
can this be a good thing for a healthy relationship?

*The difference between the right word and almost the right word
is the difference between lightning and a lightning bug.*
–Mark Twain

Communication can make or break nearly every relationship. **In
order to be defined as "healthy communication," it should be
clear, tactful, honest, loving, respectful, and responsible.** When
our communication lacks most (or all) of these qualities, the chanc-
es are that, instead, it has one or more of the following unhealthy
qualities: it is blaming, rude, narrow-minded, selfish, or irrespon-
sible. If we seem to be blocking clear and healthy communication,
we need to re-think our position. If someone else seems to be

blocking such communication, we need to discover the cause; for example, it may be that we are not listening as deeply as we could, or perhaps the other person is "hell-bent" on maintaining the misunderstanding.

Never waste your time trying to explain your thoughts and
beliefs to those who are committed to misunderstanding
you, nor trying to explain who you are to people
who refuse to know you.
—Author unknown

The world already has enough arguments and conflicts, and more of these arguments are caused by misunderstandings than actual offenses. So it stands to reason that **we could (or should) be doing a lot more work on preventing misunderstandings *before* they happen or clearing them up once they have *begun*.** Imagine the major impact it could have on creating a more peaceful world if we all focused on accomplishing this one goal: preventing or clearing misunderstandings.

It is impossible to prevent or repair misunderstandings if both parties insist on being "right." It is also impossible to prevent or clear misunderstandings if we refuse to follow the proper guidelines for healthy communication. The prevention and clearing of possible misunderstandings begins with our internal immunity. **The less we believe we have to protect our egos by taking offensive or defensive stands, the more likely we will be able to witness peace in our communication.** There is, of course, nothing wrong with also taking *external,* practical measures to communicate as clearly as possible. For example, it is wise to let our partner know what might help us to better hear and understand them.

In every conversation, there is an initiator and a recipient. Each of these has its own crucial part and its own level of responsibility. It must be remembered, however, that **our goal is *not* to get other people to learn to communicate with love and responsibility, but, rather, to maintain our own clarity and center even when others do *not* communicate well**. Doing so can be a greater challenge and a test of our character. In fact, it might be helpful to others if we demonstrate (by being a good example) *how* to communicate differently, thereby showing them that there *are* healthier ways to communicate.

The hearing that is only in the ears is one thing. The hearing of the understanding is another. But the hearing of the spirit is not limited to any one faculty, to the ear, or to the mind. Hence it demands the emptiness of all the faculties. And when the faculties are empty, then the whole being listens. There is then a direct grasp of what is right there before you that can never be heard with the ear or understood with the mind.

–Chuang Tzu

STEPS FOR HEALTHY COMMUNICATION
THE INITIATOR

- **Accentuate the positives**: Start the conversation by building some connection and appreciation for one another. For example, let the other person know what you appreciate about him/her or what is working well between you, which is why you would like to nurture an even better communicating experience.

- **Use "I" or "we" statements and be tactful**: This encourages the recipient not to feel attacked. Whenever we say or imply the word "you," it tends to create defensiveness in others, which is counterproductive to healthy communication.

- **Express your own personal "feelings," rather than "facts"**: This allows you, the initiator, to remain responsible. Also, when we speak from our feelings, we tend to be more truthful than when we speak from facts.

- **Avoid words like "always," "never," (etc.)**: It is technically impossible for anyone or anything to *always* be right or *never* be wrong. For example, it is virtually impossible that someone "never" listens to you; they have to have heard *something* from you at least once.

- **Share the "real" truth and nothing but the truth**: Before you speak, ask yourself if your words will add to, or take away from, your connection to the other person. Also ask yourself if what you are about to say is true, loving, and necessary. If not, then don't say it.

THE RECIPIENT

- **Listen**: Be sure to remain present and listen as attentively as possible.

- **Acknowledge**: Make eye contact, nod your head in acknowledgment, and/or possibly make short verbal acknowledgments that you are listening and observing whatever is being said.

- **Let them know that you might understand why they feel as they do**: This is the toughest step of all because it means letting others know that you understand where they are coming from—even if it means risking your position in the conversation.

- **Apologize when necessary**: It is not always necessary to do so, but it is good and very healthy to apologize and make amends whenever it is appropriate. Apologizing, however, does not mean begging for someone's forgiveness. A healthy apology might take the form of saying, "I am really sorry about that. That certainly was not my intention. But I totally understand why I may have come across that way." Of course, our ego would prefer that we not take responsibility like this, but we have to make a decision between "being right or being happy."

- **Ask if the "initiator" has any suggestions that might help the situation**: This is a good way to demonstrate open-mindedness. Also, it helps to create a healthy, mutual, and constructive dialogue. You might say something like, "Do you have any ideas on how we might prevent this from happening again?"

If, when practicing these rules of healthy communication, we discover that we are not able to follow these guidelines, it is wise to let the other person (or persons) know that we simply are not able to "hear" them at this time. We can take a break and try again later, after we have had time to consider why we are stumbling, or are not able to handle the conversation in a healthy manner. **As our spiritual awareness grows and we develop greater patience and tolerance, we will discover that it becomes easier to maneuver through the steps of healthy communication.**

One thing is certain: **in most disagreements, everyone simply wants to be heard.** The aforementioned steps for healthy communication allow people to be heard and to express what they are feeling, without actually drawing a conclusion about which one is "right." This is because being "right" is not the goal of healthy communication, nor is it as important as creating connection between or among people, wherein all parties are more likely to feel heard.

ADDITIONAL PRINCIPLES
OF HEALTHY COMMUNICATION

- **Be aware**: The first principle of good, clear communication is to know *why* you want to have clarity and harmony. In other words, what is your motivation? If love, respect, and/or the desire to create connection are the motivations, then you are almost certain to succeed.

- **Be responsible**: 1) Watch for your part in the challenges.   2) Take quiet time apart when needed. 3) Know when to speak and not speak. 4) Use healthy means of releasing troublesome feelings. 5) Stay out of the blame mode.

- **Be flexible**: 1) Ask yourself, "Do I want to be right or happy?" 2) Ask yourself, "What will happen if I insist on being heard and or right?" 3) Ask yourself what they might *really* want beneath their words or actions.

- **Share affection**: 1) Learn how to demonstrate affection without words. 2) Smile, touch, hug, etc. 3) Practice sharing random acts of kindness.

HEALTHY REMINDERS FOR
RESOLVING CONFLICTS

- Take responsibility.
- Avoid taking things personally.
- Practice patience.
- Honor needs.
- Honor feelings.
- Communicate clearly.
- Hold to boundaries.

- Avoid power struggles.
- Give room; do not pin down.
- Use good reasoning.
- Be open to all possible solutions.
- Identify the problem whenever possible.
- When the problem is not seen, (and even if it is) surrender it (let it go).
- Look for "win-win" or "greater good" solutions.

Qualities that Build Communication & Intimacy	Qualities that Destroy Communication & Intimacy
Trust	Distrust
Tolerance	Fault finding
Safety	Fear
Mutual power	Controlling behavior
Patience	Nagging
Love	Hurt
Tenderness	Obsessiveness
Boundaries	Addictions
Empathy	Detachment
Responsibility	Blaming Others

CHECKING-IN EXERCISE

One of the best, and simplest, exercises for improving communication is this "Checking-In Exercise," suggested by many couples' counselors. Similar to taking a pulse of ourselves, each other, and the relationship, this exercise (which only takes 10-20 minutes) helps couples to stay in touch with the condition of their relationship, as well as helping them feel safe enough to eventually discuss *anything* and *everything*. Also, it offers a safe space wherein each person can be heard, and this alone can increase the couple's sense of value and safety with one another. Couples who take a regular pulse of their relationship by doing this "Checking-In Exercise" often find the benefits to be immeasurable.

1. After creating privacy with no possibility of interruptions, the couple (or group, family, etc.) sits facing one another.

2. The "rules of engagement" must be clearly established, which include not interrupting the person whose turn it is to speak.

3. Decide who goes first as the speaker and who first will be the listener.

4. Begin by briefly sharing something (or some things) you appreciate about each other or about any positive changes going on in the relationship.

5. Then share updates with each other, which can be any new insights, revelations, epiphanies, or anything that happens to be going on in your life—major or minor.

6. Share ideas about what changes might help the relationship grow to another level—including sharing any needs that might be helpful to have met.

7. Next, if it is agreeable, the silent person can now ask questions—as long as there are clear rules about what can be asked and exactly how honest the answers will be.

8. End by complimenting and extending thanks for everything that was shared/communicated and perhaps exchange an embrace.

9. Switch roles and allow the other person to have his or her turn, following the same rules.

CHAPTER FIFTEEN

Intimacy & Affection

Intimacy is a natural expression of love-based relationships and is one of the most effective means of demonstrating love on a physical level. Intimacy means "connection" or the desire to "feel connected" with others. *Intimacy* is often a word that is broken down to mean "in-to-me-see," which implies being vulnerable enough to be seen, on all levels, by another person.

Intimacy can also include healthy acts of affection such as that of healing touch. There are numerous ways that healers have transformed the health and lives of their clients by the simple, yet profound, effects of safe, kind affection. As a healing tool, the use of affection needs no technical training and is as natural as creation itself. In fact, affection is possibly the world's most underrated method of healing.

The forms that affection can take can vary from person to person and moment to moment. This ultimately depends on the inspiration that comes to the person extending the affection and the needs of the person receiving it. And, **although the forms of authentic affection vary greatly, the inspiration and intention behind it is always the same: a symbolic expression of unconditional love.** In fact, it is actually the unconditional love behind the gesture that does the healing and not the act of affection itself.

Although intimacy may *include* sexuality (when it is appropriate), some people interpret the concept of intimacy to be the same as sexuality. However, intimacy is actually so much more because there are many ways to express affection *with* physical contact, yet *without* sexual involvement. In fact, **there are far more methods of expressing affection *without* actual physical contact than there are *with* such contact.**

Physical affection without having sex can take many forms that include a neck rub, a hug, a comforting hand on the shoulder, cuddling, and so forth. Affection without physical contact also can take a variety of forms that include, for example, a kind smile or word, a listening ear, and even the paying of a bill or the handing of a tissue to someone who is crying.

No matter what form affection may take, it plays an important role in human interaction. Behind all of our human problems lies the belief that we are separate from the love, peace, and joy of God. As a result, we feel a core level of angst, emptiness, and low self-worth. However, **when we see our brothers and sisters suffering and we choose to push through the crowd of those who are willing to let them remain in such pain and limited beliefs about themselves, we demonstrate a higher belief that they are worthy of love and care.** We can demonstrate this with some appropriate form of affection, which, in turn, shatters the limiting false beliefs that once kept them bound.

Our affectionate expressions of love (in whatever appropriate form) help them to reprogram their former beliefs that they are unloved and unlovable—thus undeserving of anyone's care. Our random acts of kindness prove that they are indeed valuable. **Our love-based, spiritual affection provides an opportunity for our brothers and sisters to accept within themselves a new level of love and self-worth.**

Nevertheless, there *are* a few potential risks involved, which include the following:

First, **when deciding how *much* affection to give or receive and in what *form* (under the above stated circumstances), we must always ask ourselves if our intentions are based on unconditional love.**

There is a story of the Hindu Master Krishna who was out for a walk with one of his consorts—Radha. Since Krishna was very handsome and spiritually powerful, many of the men were jealous of him, but the women adored him. So any woman would love to have been picked to walk with Krishna, but on this day he chose Radha. Knowing the other women would feel envious, Radha pushed her luck and asked Krishna for permission to ride on his back. He gave her permission, and as she jumped up into the air, he disappeared, and she fell to the ground. She knew immediately what she had done: she had tried to make herself special and above all others in the eyes of her Lord. She cried out for forgiveness, and Krishna then reappeared and began walking with Radha as though nothing had happened.

There are many lessons and layers of symbolism to this story. Krishna symbolizes God, who loves us and offers to walk with us, forgiving and forgetting our silly acts of egotism. Radha symbolizes our limited, human nature that should refrain from trying to be falsely "special"—the part of us that so easily gets caught up in our ego and loses sight of giving and receiving unconditional love.

Second, **as the giver, or initiator, of affection we must be able to keep our own needs and unhealed issues out of the picture**—often more easily said than done.

Third, **when expressing affection to someone, we must remain aware that it can sometimes cause more harm than good**—even when our intentions are righteous.

For example, this unfortunate possibility can occur if the recipient interprets (or confuses) our affection as either a romantic statement or a replay of some former trauma that, in fact, lacked love-based affection. In either case, the giver of affection suddenly might become misperceived as a negative image by the recipient. One of the best securities against such hazards is to remind ourselves of our original inspired intentions and to clearly communicate these intentions. Then, and only then, can we be certain that we are acting as a messenger of love and self-worth to those in need of a reminder that, indeed, they are worthy of love. Nevertheless, people will interpret the experience through their own eyes and, potentially, their unhealed issues.

We see things not as they are but as we are.

–the Talmud

There is a well-known Buddhist story that explains very well how two or more people can have the same experience; however, one may see it through eyes of purity and the other(s) through the eyes of judgment. It is the story of two monks who are on a journey. At some point in their travels, they come to a river and need to cross. They notice a woman who also needs to cross the river. So one of the monks picks her up, carries her across, and sets her down when it is safe to do so. After crossing the river, the monks begin walking again, and the second monk is noticeably disturbed. So, after a while, the first monk asks his traveling companion what is bothering him. The second monk reminds him that they are monks, and therefore he should not have touched nor carried the woman. The first monk, however, tells the second monk that, although he put the woman down many miles ago, the second monk is still carrying her.

Given the potential risks, and, therefore, trying to remain safe themselves, most people choose not to bother helping others. But **if we stand in the light of love, we might all learn to muster up the courage to help our brothers and sisters despite the potential risks.** Otherwise, we could end up like those folks who shut their doors and windows when they hear a person crying for help in the street—choosing to ignore them and not "get involved."

You might recall the popular actress who was being attacked on the street in front of her apartment. She was stabbed multiple times, but nobody was doing anything to help her. Finally, one guy set aside his own fears and thoughts of himself and restrained her assailant, thus saving her life.

Of course, one out of every-so-many people whom we offer to help will decline our offer or even accuse us of a wrong-doing, but isn't it worth the risk, given the number of people whose lives we may change forever?

The following list offers a few concepts that will assist in developing greater intimacy in relationships:

- Kind Words
- Vulnerability
- Responsibility
- Healthy, responsible communication
- Making others feel desired and desirable
- Random acts of kindness and physical affection

PART FIVE

Other Essentials About Relationships

CHAPTER SIXTEEN

Do You Really
Want to Be Special?

If there is one thing that most often makes or breaks our relationships (in every form), it is our ability (or inability) to take responsibility. As the ancient adage instructs, "Know thyself!" In order to truly be responsible, it is necessary to truly know "thyself." This goal can be accomplished at two levels: spiritual and human. If we know ourselves spiritually, we will of course know our Divinity, which, in itself, would make our lives complete. However, even if we fall short of this spiritual level of self-knowledge, just knowing our *human* selves and what makes us act and react the way we do, can (in and of itself) completely change our relationships with others, because (despite having many strengths), as we become aware of our "weaknesses" we can choose not to indulge them. Furthermore, if we truly know ourselves as human beings, we will know and understand how our interactions with others are affected by our unhealed wounds, as well as our perceived "needs." And the greatest of these needs is to be "special."

The problem begins whenever we (on levels known or unknown) doubt our Divinity—our state of being Unconditional Love. Doubting our True Nature (consciously or unconsciously), causes us to feel inadequate, which leads us to search for people or things that might compensate by making us feel "special." Now everyone around us will unknowingly be assigned the duty of "making us feel special." In other words, we need a "special" feeling for (or from) some-one or some-thing to make us "tingle inside" in an attempt to make up for the bliss we lost when we forgot who we are,

Not remembering how to feel *Unconditional* Love, we at-tempt to replace it with a *conditional* form of *false* love, called "specialness." We become attracted to people who will like us, support us, and stroke our egos in the ways we think we need, in an effort to feel more complete or special. Since other people can make us feel special only for a limited time, we eventually feel at-tacked or rejected when they seem to change the behavior we so desperately needed from them. We may even try to prevent these rude awakenings, or let-downs, by clinging tenaciously to these other people or by bargaining to keep the relationship alive, just so we will not have to confront the loss of this false sense of spe-cialness. That is why such relationships often are referred to as un-healthy and codependent. Although these are the people we would classify as people we "love" or "like," unfortunately, this view will change when they no longer fulfill our need for feeling special.

We also encounter people who, for whatever reason, refuse to give us the feeling of specialness for which we thirst. These are gen-erally the people in our lives that we *don't* like. Not only do these individuals fail to make us feel special, they, undoubtedly, make us feel very "un-special." For example, when other drivers refuse to let us into traffic, we are offended because they failed to make us feel special by allowing us to cut in. When we want to engage in a conversation or power struggle with others, but they will not par-ticipate, we then feel ignored or disempowered. When our partners refuse to give us sex, they fail to make us feel special and desired.

When a mother chooses to share affection with her child, the father may feel that his specialness is threatened. Even children, who seem so innocent, will battle with their siblings to gain the special attention or approval of their parents and cry if they do not get what they want.

Most people might assume that it is normal or even healthy to want to feel special to others or to allow others to be special to us. But beware! **Hidden behind all forms of specialness (which always include conditions) lurks the need to compensate for a lack of feeling Unconditional Love—*for* others or *from* others**.

One way to recognize our dysfunctional need to feel special is to observe our relationships and notice when we feel insecure about our value, or how desirable we feel. We might also notice how much we compare ourselves to (or compete with) others and how often we participate in power struggles. And, we can observe how we feel and react when someone doesn't say or give us something we feel we need. These are all signs that we believe we lack wholeness and are therefore trying to compensate by desperately seeking a feeling of specialness. Eventually, we discover that our tactics will not work and, in fact, may even push others away—thus increasing our angst and making us feel even less special.

The desire to feel special is such a primal, egotistic need that even animals attack each other for roles of dominance—a form of specialness. One might assume that, given the negative repercussions of living with such a desperate need for specialness, we would want to give it up. However, the ego tells us that if we give up the desire to be special, we are "losing something," and the ego has all the evidence of an ego-based world to support its case.

For example, the ego plants such negative feelings as loneliness (or the fear of being alone) in our emotional body. Then, if someone ends a relationship with us (which may actually be a healthy thing for us), the ego triggers that emotion of loneliness to support the idea that the other person's rejection of us made us feel upset. Since we have forgotten our Divine Nature (which is the real reason why we feel alone and upset), we buy into the false conclusion that we must *need* that other person to feel whole, lovable, and of course, special. Obviously **none of the ideas that feed our insatiable thirst for specialness are true, but they will seem valid until we choose to remember our True Identity and are willing to go through the "drug-like" withdrawals of purging ourselves from the ego's addictive hold.**

Each time we have a feeling of ego-based specialness, it is a victory for the ego, and the casualties include everyone involved. The pursuit of specialness, like any addiction, is always at the cost of inner peace. As soon as we manage to stake out an ounce of specialness in our lives, we will wage wars to protect it, or keep it, thus losing peace and connection with our True Identity.

The teachings of Buddha and *A Course in Miracles (ACIM)* both explain that all forms of specialness that we assign to others result in attachments, including the attachment to preserving our feeling of specialness. Since the very thing or person we are attached to will, in time, either change or disappear, the specialness always ends in some form of suffering. Although in Truth, we are safe, resting in God, according to *ACIM*, "our specialness . . . is attacked by everything that walks and breathes."

Therefore, **if we want peace of mind, we will do the necessary work to transform our relationships from being conditional (contingent on being made to feel special) to being unconditional (contingent on nothing).** In effect, the latter reminds us that we are loved by God, complete within ourselves, and have no *needs* for anyone to fill. From this level of understanding and responsibility, we realize that any uncertainty we may have about these truths will be mirrored in our relationships, showing us where we still have work to do.

If specialness were a flowering weed, its roots would be the belief that we are separate from God. Its stem would be desperation, and its flower would be specialness. The flower of specialness, of course, blooms to get attention and dies soon after. Then its "fragrance" (or lingering scent) would be the resulting codependent relationships. The stem of desperation not only supports the flower of specialness but also (being so distressed) will cause us to feel fear, hyper-defensiveness, jealousy, and conditional love—all of which are rooted in the erroneous thinking that we are separate from God and from each other.

Once we have defined who we are through the conditional love or ego-based needs of our relationships, we have replaced the freedom and joy found only in Unconditional Love with the unquenchable need to feel special. In so doing, we will not be capable of truly knowing one another. Instead, we will know others only through our perceptions of who we *want* them to be. These perceptions are rooted in what we believe we *need* from them, which, likewise, is rooted in who we believe we are. **The more limited we believe ourselves to be, the more limitations we will need to place on others**.

Perceiving ourselves as ego-based persons, we will determine, or define, who we are by what we get from the outer world—which is part of the dysfunction of codependence. Also, we will feel continually threatened or affected by what other people say or do. Consequently, the actions, feelings, and comments of others then will threaten our perceived reality and our sense of specialness. This perceived threat may feel so unbearable that we grab yet another person to help us deal with the pain by again making us feel loved, lovable, and special. And so begins another cycle of codependence that will continue to dominate how we experience life.

As much as we might wish otherwise, in actuality, we are not "special" even in the eyes of God. No one can be "special" because **God loves us ALL as ONE BEING and not as parts.** Being the Presence of Unconditional Love, God does not experience "degrees of love," such as a special love for Jesus and less love for Hitler. This may seem shocking to the ego part of us that likes to judge and thinks it needs to be special, or superior to others. Think about it, could God really love one part of Its ONE Child/Creation more than another part? This makes as much sense as trying to shampoo one hair on our head that we have a special fondness for, while ignoring and neglecting the others.

God loves us unconditionally, and specialness is the opposite of Unconditional Love, because being special is being totally conditional. Unconditional Love brings freedom; specialness offers only limitations and captivity. **Every time we create specialness, we settle for something that is not real, will not last, will bring us pain, and will confirm that we are not already loved, nor are we complete within ourselves.** If we understood this, would we really want to be special?

Fortunately, there is an answer to this dilemma. We can learn to extend love unconditionally from the core of our True Self and thereby surrender all egotistical needs to be special or to make others egotistically special to us. Ultimately, **all of our relations are the same and equally deserving of our love and kindness.** So we are destined to eventually love everyone—equally. Does this mean we should move every man, woman, and child into our home? Of course not! However, in our mind's eye we can see everyone as equal and equally deserving of love.

We can love everyone with the intention of loving them as God loves them—unconditionally—yet we are also free to decide which *forms* of love are most appropriate for each person at any given moment. So, while loving all people equally, we can also freely choose how to express that love in a way that feels right for each given scenario, which may vary from our own child to a stranger and from our partner to our friend. Even Jesus and Buddha loved *everyone* but chose to treat some of their friends and apostles differently than others.

The more we are filled with Spirit, the more complete within ourselves we will feel, thus eliminating the need for others to make us feel special. Although all relationships in this material world begin as special (being rooted in the perception that we are separate), they can be healed by forgiving the misperceptions we project onto them—thus making the relationship healed. When a relationship is healed, it becomes Holy, or Whole, or One. What is ONE cannot be special, since special—defined as "one 'part' being more exceptional than another 'part',"—requires separation. **As we choose to bring ourselves and our relationships prayerfully to the altar of Unconditional Love, asking for Spiritual Guidance on how to forgive errors and love unconditionally, all forms of specialness will evaporate before the Light of God.**

CHAPTER SEVENTEEN

Wisely Choose Your Friends

Most people have heard the saying "Choose your friends wisely." Some people translate this to mean "Choose your friends *cautiously.*" This implies the need for us to be cautious about whom we "let in" as friends, which can be good advice but can also be too rigid and end up keeping too many people at a distance. Instead, let's consider it to mean "Wisely choose friends," or friends who are healthy and mature—emotionally, psychologically, and spiritually. These criteria not only apply to others who want to be our friends but also apply to us and our need to be good friends to others.

Surround yourself with the best company, those who will inspire you and strengthen your discrimination and will power.

–Paramahansa Yogananda

We all would benefit from considering how many "true" friends we have. But before counting, we first should eliminate people who are really acquaintances and not actually friends. We also should eliminate family members and one-sided friendships (anyone whom we might consider as a friend but who does not reciprocate the title).

It is not uncommon for our list of friends to gradually get smaller as we ask a few important questions. But whoever remains on the list deserves our gratitude and appreciation, as they probably are true friends who have been there for us when we needed them.

If your list, however, lacks an abundance of true friends, it might be worth considering some of the most common reasons, which are as follows:

- You have too many unhealed wounds and are possibly too selective or have distanced yourself from potential friends.

- You are not yet spiritually or psychologically healthy enough for others to feel a safe, close bond with you.

- You, yourself, have failed to be a true friend or failed to demonstrate the characteristics of a true, healthy friend.

- You are too busy with work, family, or other distractions to have close, true friends (which may be an excuse that conceals other issues).

- Sometimes, however, you have few true friends because you have made *healthier* choices in your life and have found it helpful to no longer spend time with, or befriend, people who do not reflect your higher good.

In general, true friends often see the "worst" side of us (as well as revealing the worst side of themselves) and are willing to not take it personally. In fact, **true friends do not allow judgmental thoughts to replace feelings of love and appreciation**. Instead, they are healthy and strong enough to "call us" on our "stuff," while tactfully and lovingly encouraging us to do healing work.

We can have open, honest, and thorough communication with our true friends, wherein we exchange our darkest secrets and greatest dreams, knowing that what we share will be kept confidential and not turned into gossip or used against us. This is because **a true friend is a *spiritual* friend, and a spiritual friend is responsible and respectful.**

> *In divine friendship there is ever-increasing respect; each one thinks only of the highest welfare of the other.*
> **–Paramahansa Yogananda**

True friends do not overtly or covertly take out their issues on one another. Instead, true friendships are sacred spaces wherein people are committed to growth and authenticity. This involves a commitment to removing their ego-based masks and being open and vulnerable with each other. It also means that if or when the ego rears its ugly head, healthy people will apologize and make amends as soon as possible. Anything less, occurring consistently, is neither healthy nor a true friendship.

A healthy relationship and true friendship is always *increasing* in the quantity and quality of Spirit flowing through it on a day-to-day basis. Therefore, a *decrease* in the presence of Spirit might indicate that the relationship is immature, unhealthy, and is not a sacred experience.

One day, all human beings will recognize that they are "Soul Mates" with *all* other souls. But, first we must transform *hurtful* relationships into *healed* relationships. Then these healed relationships can become Soul Mate relationships. While we are transforming our relationships, it helps to have allies, or healthy friendships, rooted in our "friendship" with Spirit. This primary relationship makes easier our journey towards healing all other relationships.

What you seek is seeking you.

–Rumi

As we evolve, our friendships become purposeful and less shallow. Also we learn to choose, or gravitate towards, friends that resonate with love and self-worth, rather than adding to our doubts and fears. Meanwhile, we remember that, like romantic relationships, friendships do not just "happen;" they are grown. Jesus taught that, ultimately, true friends are people who would give up their lives for us. His reference was not necessarily to people who literally would "die" for us, but to people who would set aside their egos for us and for the sake of true friendship.

Unfortunately, as with romantic relationships, when we commit to creating a better life and increasing our sense of self-worth, **sometimes our present friendships cannot make the transition from our "old" way of living and into our "new" way of being**. During such times of transition, it is crucial to be loving and responsible, as well as aware of what is occurring. Often the people involved become irritated; and triggered by the change or the seeming failure of the relationship, they take it out on each other. However, if we are aware of what is happening, we can choose to act or react differently, based on the understanding that although we may have been good friends (or partners), our energies or personality types are no longer compatible.

Additionally, in our friendships (and other relationships), we need to be careful not to allow *minor* issues to become *major* issues that divide us. It is easy to slip into the ego's mindset of finding fault with others—including friends. But is the fault truly unbearable? If so, then perhaps it is best to part ways. But what if the issue is minor and we simply assume (out of ignorance) that it is major. Could we not overlook the issue, if we take time to realize that perhaps it makes up only ten percent of an otherwise rewarding relationship?

Nevertheless, if some relationships (family, friends, partners) just can't seem to make the transition from the past (unhealthy) to the present (healthy), and we are clear that we have done everything we can to improve matters, but with insufficient success; then such relationships may need to be cut loose and surrendered to God.

It is important to remember, however, that **everything appearing on the "outside"—including our friendships—mirrors how we are doing on the "inside."** If we separate from others with resentment or hurt, our unfaced challenges and unlearned lessons are certain to go with us. However, if we separate with love and responsibility (parting ways with an attitude of unconditional love), we are doing all that Spirit asks of us. Then our future relationships are destined to go well—provided we keep the faith.

If we die today, **what matters on the other side is not how many people we once mistakenly _called_ friends, but how many people were _true_ friends, or holy relationships.** So, we must learn to wisely choose our friends, while excluding no one from the Unconditional Love in our hearts.

CHAPTER EIGHTEEN

Soul Mates & Twin Souls

A "Soul Mate" relationship is very similar to a healed and holy relationship. It is an ongoing relation with another individual (or individuals) with whom we connect again and again in various times and places to support each other in our soul growth. Soul Mates are numerous and are simply mates (or friends) with whom we feel a common affinity. The Soul Mates in any given lifetime might include our parents, children, friends, family, work associates, and/or intimate partners.

A Soul Mate is not to be confused with the term "Twin Soul" or "Twin Flame," which is often mistakenly interpreted to be someone who is the "other half" of our "divided" soul. This, by definition, implies that we are not complete beings, which is simply not true. Unfortunately, the notion that there is someone "out there" who can "complete us" becomes easy bait for our inner "romantic" who longs for the perfect, storybook ending: meeting the "perfect person" with whom we can live happily ever after.

In truth, "Twin Soul" relationships have a purpose beyond romance and involve a specific one (or more) of our Soul Mates with whom we have chosen to join (in a spiritual partnership) to share a common purpose (a spiritual contract), usually for the "greater good" of humanity. In other words, **although Twin Souls can** *choose* **to be romantically involved, they usually come to-**

gether in order to fulfill some important *work* that they have in common. But the priority is usually focused on "the work" (or the mission or purpose). This joint purpose usually is meant to have some—small or large—positive effect in the world or in people's lives.

For example, Helen Schucman (the scribe of *A Course in Miracles*) was the Twin Soul of her co-editor, Bill Thetford, while being a Soul Mate to her husband. Also, Edgar Cayce's Twin Soul was not his wife but his stenographer Gladys Davies, who made it possible to record his readings for the good of humanity. Jesus of Nazareth and his mother, Mary, shared a common purpose and were Twin Souls, as she brought him forth to heal the world. And, as close as both Lennon and McCartney were to their (Soul Mates) wives, they were Twin Souls with each other.

Soul Mate and Twin Soul relationships each have their own unique purpose, and both have an ongoing influence upon one another. One of the primary distinctions between these two types of relationships is that **Soul Mates are brought together in order to assist both *individuals* in soul growth, while Twin Souls often come together in a joint task to achieve an outcome that serves the greater whole of *humanity*.** And, incidentally, although all Twin Souls begin as Soul Mates, not all Soul Mates become Twin Souls.

Soul Mate relations do not occur merely by chance; instead they are fueled, or determined, by a Divine purpose for the growth of all individuals involved. There are no accidents or chance encounters. Soul Mates are drawn together in the present because they have been together in the past (even previous lives). And, although Twin Souls have a specific purpose or contract, Soul Mate relationships are between seemingly ordinary people who share an *extraordinary* connection.

The two of you are reflections of each other, the One God mas-
querading as two bodies, two minds, two hearts.
–Joyce and Barry Vissell

We not only experience individual Soul Mate connections, but also connections with groups of people with whom we have worked, lived, and fought beside. Larger Soul Mate groupings have a tremendous impact upon the people involved, as well as within the community (or world) in which they live.

One of our primary purposes for being on Earth is to create healthy, Soul Mate relationships with everyone in our lives. All such relationships have the potential to be helpful experiences in terms of soul growth and personal transformation simply because we learn the most about ourselves by interacting with others. Furthermore, **the soul already possesses a pattern of perfection within itself just waiting to be awakened, which usually occurs through our deepest Soul Mate relationships**. This awakening marks the point where a Soul Mate relationship becomes a healed and holy relationship.

For in your longing for love, you recognize as well
your longing for your Self.
–Mari Perron and Dan Odegard

Eventually, as humanity reaches a unified consciousness (without separation), all souls will feel like Soul Mates because all relationships will become healed and holy. In fact, the more each soul becomes whole, the more able it is to connect with other souls. Again, individuals are attracted to one another as Soul Mates primarily to provide the other with the impetus to become whole. From this perspective, the story of Soul Mates is really the story of each soul's search for Wholeness or Holiness. In other words, **our search for our Soul Mate or Twin Soul actually is a symbolic expression of our search for God and our return to oneness with each other**. However, true Wholeness can be realized only as the soul reawakens to its True Spiritual Source.

CHAPTER NINETEEN

What About Sexuality?

We often perceive sensuality and physical intimacy as experiences of the material world that are the opposite of spiritual or transcendental experiences. However, our physical self is, in fact, meant to be experienced in harmony *with* our spiritual self, since to judge a part is to judge the whole. As one of the early Church Fathers said, "That which is not *lived* is not redeemed." This means that if we judge or avoid our human sexuality, then our sexuality remains unredeemed.

Most spiritual masters have dealt with the topic of sexuality (including their own sexuality) in one of two ways: 1) sexual desires were transformed until they were lessened or eliminated altogether; or 2) a healthy, balanced life was chosen wherein intimacy was no more, nor less, important than any other aspects of human life.

Generally, our spirit rules our soul, and our ego rules our body. This means we have two opposing kingdoms within that are vying for complete control. **If we let the body's biological "needs" control us, we are being run by the ego, which is trying to squash our soul.** However, if we choose to diminish our ego's impact and allow our spirit and soul to take over, then our ego-based urges and impulses (that seem to control us) can be replaced with the soul's love and inspiration. The body then can become a vehicle with which we express that love. Although we still will feel passion and excitement, these emotions are now love-based *feelings*, instead of ego-based *compulsions*.

Most of us know that the greatest gift is the gift of love. But many of us do not realize that one of the deepest expressions of love is intimacy and that **sexuality is one of the most powerful physical expressions of both love *and* intimacy.** Therefore, *who, how, when* and *where* we share this expression is something worth deep consideration.

> *When sex is just an unconscious, mechanical urge in you, it is wrong. Remember, sex is not wrong: the mechanicalness of it is wrong. If you can bring some light of intelligence into your sexuality, that light will transform it. It will not be sexuality any more—it will be something totally different, so different that you don't have a word for it. In the East we have a word for it, 'Tantra'. In the West you don't have any word for it. When sex becomes joined together, is yoked with intelligence, a totally new energy is created—that energy is called Tantra.*
>
> —Osho

There are three primary active forces (or types of love) within the human consciousness that assist us in expressing and experiencing the most profound level of relationships with others. These forces are as follows: 1) Love (with the heart), 2) Desire (with our feelings or emotions), and 3) Passion or Sexuality (with the body). Most people find themselves experiencing one or two of these active forces. Yet, the ideal scenario is to have all three of these forces in harmonious balance.

Heart Love (agape) is selfless and universal and refers to love at the level of the heart and soul. Before we are able to share love from the heart and soul, however, we need to evolve spiritually to the point where we can maintain this soul-level of consciousness and think beyond our ego-selves. In order to share love at this level, we must be brave and courageous enough to risk vulnerability at its deepest level.

Emotional love (desire) can serve as a bridge between love and sex, or between the heart and the body. The type (and level) of desire that we feel can accurately gage how much quality and spontaneity we have in our lives and our relationships. Desire can act as kindling for a healthy form of the fire of passion—particularly if that desire stems from a developed friendship, playfulness, and respect. Yet, desire alone (without being founded and inspired in higher and deeper forms of love) often causes feelings of longing and neediness.

Passionate love (affection or sexuality) are best when accompanied by love and healthy desire; combined, they can create one of the most profound demonstrations of manifesting love and Heaven on Earth. In its healthiest, sensual manifestation, love is often referred to as "Sacred Sexuality." In Sacred Sexuality, the bodies meet to physically express what is felt in the heart and soul. This is not to imply that all sexual experiences must be between two individuals who are "in love." Instead, each person learns how to be in a space of loving presence for their own benefit before joining sexually with another. This, in turn, can bring a sacred union to both.

When we greet love, life, and others from/with a healthy balance of the three aspects of love, desire and sexual passion, we are then able to share the greatest gift of our true self with our chosen partners. Then, we will be in a position to receive the same gift from them in return. For a healthy sharing at this depth of intimacy, emotional and spiritual maturity is needed. If such maturity is present, we intuitively will choose the right partners, those who have, in essence, the emotional maturity and readiness to match ours.

Although sensual pleasure is a part of sexuality, it should be a *result* and not a *goal*. Once we know that we are in a space of love, safety, responsibility, and healthy communication, then we can let go and surrender to true pleasure—healthy pleasure. If we try to surrender to pleasure without the requirements of love and respect (which are expansive) being met and experienced, then we often end up feeling empty, hurt, or ashamed (which is constrictive).

Most intimate/sexual relationships are ego-based. Ego-based sex is controlling, needy, possessive, and goal oriented—which is why it often ends (at best) in the shallowest forms of orgasm. Sacred Sexuality, on the other hand, is an expression of love, respect, appreciation, and freedom—which is why it can be expanded into the deepest forms of orgasm.

Since a true sexual union is harmonious, it is important to understand that complete cooperation, communication, and agreement between both partners are a must. If the two are truly one, then there will be sensitivity for the likes and dislikes of each partner. In effect, **sexual union can enhance both partners' compassion and sensitivity with themselves and each other.**

Feeling safe is a vital part of a relationship. Possessiveness does not create a feeling of safety. In fact, the more we lack a feeling of safety, the more we will become possessive and insecure. So, **if we create more love and respect in our partnerships, we will feel more secure and safe and then will be less possessive.** However, this does not mean we will become weak or permissive toward a partner's infidelity. Such behavior can result in feelings of being unloved and unsafe in a relationship, which means the relationship has become unhealthy.

If you love a flower, don't pick it up. Because if you pick it up it dies and it ceases to be what you love. So if you love a flower, let it be. Love is not about possession. Love is about appreciation.

–Osho

Sacred Sexuality, however, creates a feeling of safety. An ancient art of sensuality combined with spirituality, Sacred Sexuality includes many (but not all) forms of "Tantra." Most of the arts of sexuality (existing in many cultures) include numerous rituals and techniques. Tantra, for example, typically incorporates yoga, diet, prayer, and meditation. Some forms of Tantra also embrace various sexual practices, including intercourse. Beyond the external techniques, however, the *internal* aspects of true Tantra begin in the mind and heart as the intention of authentic love and respect (or honoring) between practitioners. Concerning the *external* aspects of true Tantra, all of the rituals and sexual positions can be summarized as follows: "take your time . . . move slowly and deeply—in mind, body, and soul." **All true forms of Sacred Sexuality encourage partners to move slowly enough to remain connected on all levels—which is always made easier when there are mutual, authentic feelings of love and respect**. Although some people may experience fast and "hot" sex without any true feelings of love, such encounters cannot compare with the slow and "warm" experience of sex with authentic feelings of love and respect. In other words, when we practice true Tantra, we feel love in our hearts, while encouraging our bodies to move in synch with each other.

Lovers don't finally meet somewhere.
They're in each other all along.

–Rumi

Ultimately, the goal of any true form of Sacred Sexuality is to experience each thought, feeling, and sensation with as much presence as possible. Then, **we seem to disappear and, for a little while, enter Heaven where there are no bodies. Therefore, we are no longer "making love" but instead, we *become* the love we were once making**.

CHAPTER TWENTY

What is True Love?

Although there is really only One world, or One reality—God's—in our world of duality, we seem to have *two* realities, which are as follows: **In Spirit, everything is Eternal, Unlimited, and Unconditional—including Love. Therefore, Divine Love is Eternal, Unlimited, and Unconditional.** On Earth, however, everything changes, is limited, and is conditional—including love. Consequently, human love is fleeting, limited, and conditional. The development of spiritual love, true love, unconditional love, should therefore be our goal.

> *According to those who know man's whole being—his mind, his heart and his being—love has to be an expression of your being, not an emotion. Emotion is very gradual, very changing. One moment it seems that is all. Another moment you are simply empty. So the first thing to do is to take love out of this crowd of overwhelming emotions. Love is not overwhelming. On the contrary, love is a tremendous insight, clarity, sensitivity, and awareness. But that kind of love rarely exists, because very few people ever reach to their being.*
>
> —Osho

With the difference between the two options (real love and conditional love) being so obvious, it would seem like a "no-brainer" as

to which one most people would choose to experience. Nevertheless, most human beings (consciously or unconsciously) choose to
repeat, over and over again, the experience of limited, conditional
love in their relationships.

When attempting to define "Unconditional Love," we often try
to make Unconditional Love fit within human references. But, as
soon as there is a "you" trying to define what love is OR *whom* to
love, *how* to love, and *what* to love, we are doomed to fall short of
truly loving *unconditionally*. On one level, this is perfectly under-
standable, as we can do only the best we are capable of at the moment (or from our present awareness).

> *True love has no object. Many speak of their unconditional love
> for another. Unconditional love is the experience of being; there
> is no 'I' and 'other,' and anyone or anything it touches is experi-
> enced in love. You cannot unconditionally love someone. You can
> only be unconditional love. It is not a dualistic emotion. It is a
> sense of oneness with all that is. The experience of love arises
> when we surrender our separateness into the universal. It is a
> feeling of unity. You don't love another, you are another.*
>
> –Stephen Levine

Ultimately, to truly understand Unconditional Love, we
need to embody this Love. This awareness of Unconditional
Love can be realized by accessing our Divinity—which may
seem to be out of reach at times. So, until we maintain this level
of Divinity, on a consistent basis, it is best to practice Unconditional
Love on a level that is as close as possible to being Divine. In other
words, although presently we might be unable to *totally* understand
Unconditional Love (unless we are in our Divinity), we can, in the
meantime, experience glimpses of its essence.

When you love purely,
you know God whether you realize it or not.

–Mari Perron and Dan Odegard

Unconditional Love is *not* an emotion; it is a Divine State of Being. To love unconditionally means to Love as God Loves. Therefore, unconditional love cannot be for only *some* people or for some *parts* of some people. Nor can it come from only *some* parts of us, such as physical or emotional, and not from *other* parts. Unconditional Love is not there on *some* days and gone on *others*. Since it is a Divine state, it must be as eternally present as God Itself. Therefore, if we have love for someone or something and it fails to meet this criterion, it is probably not unconditional. **If our love for someone or something is ever conditional in any way, then it is not a true expression of Love Divine.** Nevertheless, our ability to love unconditionally will increase as we continue to grow spiritually.

Can't two people be in love and both be so intelligent and so
sensitive that there is freedom and absence of a center that makes
for conflict? The feeling of being in love is utterly without conflict.
There is no loss of energy in being in love. The loss of energy is
in the tail, in everything that follows—jealousy, possessiveness,
suspicion, doubt, the fear of losing that love, the constant demand
for reassurance and security. Surely it must be possible to func-
tion in a sexual relationship with someone you love without the
nightmare which usually follows. Of course it is.

–Krishnamurti

If we are triggered by the behaviors of other people, if we believe that we would be happier "if only" those other people behaved differently, we are witnessing the conditions we have placed on love. It is as though we were saying that if *only* they would behave differently we would feel more loved and respected by them and would then also love and respect them in return. Since this implies that love is not *already* present, such love is therefore incomplete (imperfect) and conditional. **When we make bargains for love, the love is never real and will not be long-lasting**. Needless to say, when the conditions of such bargaining wear off, we will need to create more bargains so that each of us can feel falsely loved again.

Being unconditional in our love and choices does not mean that we do not have preferences in life. It simply means that we remain as unattached as possible to the outcome of any given situation. We all are benefited by learning how to express our preferences in a healthy manner and not from a place of control or neediness. Healthy preferences are similar to having our needs met at a reasonable level. When we express our needs in the form of preferences, rather than expectations or demands, it allows for more flexibility. On the other hand, when we express our requests and become upset when they are not met, then we know that our requests were actually agendas, expectations, or attachments, and as such, inevitably result in the pain of disappointment.

Conditional love is always "dependent" (on needs being met) and exists in relationships that are "codependent." Such **false forms of love are so fleeting and volatile that they must constantly be fed by more and more flattery, approval, gifts, and bargaining.** People literally sell their bodies and souls to get even a glimpse of false, conditional love, simply because it feels better than seemingly having no love at all. But in reality, it *isn't* better. The spiritual, psychological, and physical expenses of settling for limited forms of love are far greater than the little we receive for our bargaining, or attempts to "purchase" love.

Although loving unconditionally might mean that it is our intention to see past the errors of others, it certainly does not mean we are blind to such errors. Imagine, for example, if Jesus (or any other master) had come upon a man who was about to harm a child. Would he walk past and say, "No big deal; it's just an illusion?" Of course not! Neither would he buy into the idea of making the child (the victim) right and the murderous man (the victimizer) wrong. He would know that within each, there is a Divine Essence, albeit momentarily forgotten. He would also know that both parties involved believe in the same core illusion: the man believes he is separate from God and therefore is *hurting* so much inside that he takes it out on the child; while the child also believes he is separate from God and therefore becomes *suseptable* to the abuses of the man.

So, how do we become better at practicing such a seemingly impossible task—expressing unconditional love? First, we work to heal the false belief that we are separate from God: we strengthen our connection to the Source of Unconditional Love—our True Self—which is Love Divine. Without establishing this connection to the Source of Unconditional Love, all attempts to experience true love would be futile. Once we have made this connection to Spirit, however, we are then more prepared to practice unconditional love in our day-to-day lives.

Whether or not we choose to practice deeper levels of forgiveness, one thing is certain: we cannot attain the consciousness of unconditional love just by studying or analyzing the concept or by "preaching" it to others. Instead, we must actually live it by practicing it! **We must be diligent in recognizing each time we are** either choosing not to love (judging), or we are loving with conditions. Once we have this awareness, we are free to choose to do otherwise by loving unconditionally.

> We are put on Earth a little space,
> That we may learn to bear the beams of love.
> —William Blake

Although the external *form* of unconditional love may differ with strangers we pass on the street versus our most intimate friends or partners, the inner *intention* remains the same—to allow the Divine aspect of ourselves to seek and love the Divine aspect in others. This intention is more often accomplished one step at a time, rather than in huge leaps.

When we begin to truly understand and apply unconditional love, we will find ourselves experiencing the following (and more) in nearly every form of relationship we encounter:

- Greater acceptance of others, rather than trying to change them or get something from them.
- Recognition that others are coming from either love or fear and deserving of our patience when we recognize the latter.
- Interdependence, enough to not "need" anything from others, but still willing to share whatever we have to offer, as well as receiving what others have to offer.
- Less need to "prove" anything and less need to be "right."
- Conflicts lessening in number or at least *our* participation lessens.
- Forgiving ourselves when we recognize that impatience and/or judgment have somehow surfaced.
- More love for more people and more joyful moments, which are the natural effects (gifts) that come from maintaining a holy, forgiving life.

To further understand the attributes of unconditional love, let us paraphrase the Biblical quote from Corinthians 1 regarding love:

The person who practices Unconditional Love is patient, is kind, and envies no one. The person who practices Unconditional Love is never boastful, nor conceited, nor rude; never selfish, nor quick to take offense. There is nothing a practitioner of Unconditional Love cannot face; there is no limit to his/her faith, or hope, or endurance. There are three things that last forever: faith, hope, and unconditional love; but the greatest of them all is Unconditional Love.

CHAPTER TWENTY ONE

Summary & Conclusion

This book would be a contradiction if it did not end right where it began, which is to conclude that **relationships have only one main purpose but with two parts: 1) sharing love and 2) learning about and removing all of the obstacles *to* that love.** Therefore, the focus of this book has been on creating *fulfilling* (or healthy, love-based) relationships, rather than on hype, stimulation, and techniques for how to get what we want from others.

There are two primary messages intended in this book: The first is to convey the idea that we cannot create fulfilling relationships with *others* unless we have a fulfilling relationship with *ourselves*. And we cannot have a fulfilling relationship with *ourselves* unless we have a fulfilling relationship with *Spirit*. The second message intended in this book is to explain exactly how to nurture a greater sense of fulfillment in each of our three relationships, which is done as follows:

Our relationship with God is nurtured through the practice of Communion: This involves some form of prayer and meditation in order to connect with the Divine.

Our relationship with Self is nurtured through the practice of Responsibility and Self-Awareness: This involves self-healing and having healthy boundaries, necessary to support and develop oneself.

Our relationship with Others is nurtured through the practice of Connection: This involves healthy communication and authentic forms of intimacy and affection, necessary means for joining with others.

If all the aforementioned has been conveyed in an interesting, informative, applicable manner; then the purpose of this book has been accomplished.

When all three relationships (God, Self, and Others) have been given their proper attention and nurturance, we are sure to experience, on an ongoing basis, such positive effects as a greater sense of peace and contentment. Otherwise, we are doomed to struggle with the usual life-long relationship issues.

In conclusion, to restate the core principles at the heart and soul of this book, God is Love and we are made in the image of God. Therefore, we are Love Divine. **We never were meant to "fall in love" or to "be in love." We were meant to** *be* **love.** And in *being* love, we learn to *share* that love as unconditionally as possible. This is our right, our purpose, and our destiny.

What began as a limited form of romantic love, now is Love Divine.

APPENDIX

Relationship Exercises

S ome of the following exercises have been featured earlier on in the book. However, there are some included here that are helpful additions to the ones already shared.

TRACKING EXERCISE
For people who trigger you

1. **Recognize:** Think of a person (or event) in your life that seems to trigger you and begin the exercise by saying (in your own words), "I recognize that I seem to be bothered, upset, or angered by (insert name) _____."

2. **Accept:** Repeat (aloud or to yourself): "I accept that hidden behind this person are also a few negative feelings such as (name a few emotions—e.g., resentment, shame, feeling controlled, etc.) _____." Then take a moment to see if you can identify any other people or events from your past that brought up similar emotions in you. If so, you are now seeing a "negative" pattern that has resurfaced in your current person. Note that if you had healed this issue in the *past* to the point of completion, it most likely would not be resurfacing in the *present*. This is why we often say that we never really are seeing our current relations in the "present moment," but only from a past, unhealed perspective.

3. **Surrender:** Make a sincere effort to surrender the past experience with this person or event (as well as all the negative emotions around them) to God to be given a clearer, healthier perspective and to be blessed and transformed into a Holy Relationship.

4. **Refill:** Now take 2-3 minutes to imagine drawing Light down from the ethers, through your head, and into your heart for the next several inhalations. At the same time, hear the words, *Love* and *Healing* or *Peace* and *Joy*, or whatever two words you prefer (commonly referred to as a mantra). Then, on the exhalation, simply spread the energy throughout your body as you hear the words, "And so it is."

5. **Give Thanks:** Lastly, prayerfully give thanks to God for the healing, as well as thanking whoever popped up in your exercise, since they now have given you the opportunity to recognize an unhealed memory and an unhealed pattern that you once pushed away and onto someone else. Also give thanks that you now have chosen to fill yourself with a greater abundance of God.

TRACKING EXERCISE
For people to whom you feel attracted

1. **Recognize:** Think of a person in your life whom you seem to like or are attracted to (which can also be a food, alcohol, or anything material) and begin the exercise by saying (in your own words), "I recognize that I seem to be drawn toward, or attracted to, (insert name of person or thing) _____."

2. **Accept:** Repeat (aloud or to yourself): "I accept that hidden behind this person (or thing) are also a few positive feelings such as (name a few emotions—e.g., stimulated, excited, attrac-

tive, appreciated, happy, etc.) _____."
Then take a moment to see if you can identify any other people, events, or memories from your past that brought up similar
emotions in you. If so, you are now seeing a "positive" pattern
that has resurfaced in your current person (or thing). Note that
if you had integrated this person or events in the *past* to the
point of allowing yourself to own (as your own talent) this
good characteristic, or trait, it most likely would not be resurfacing in the *present*. This is why we were told in the Ten Commandments to not "covet our neighbor's goods." What this
meant (in part) was that instead of seeing something we value
in someone else, we should absorb it and own it for ourselves.

3. **Surrender**: Make a sincere effort to surrender to God the past
choice to believe that these positive traits were not within you,
but, instead, were seen only in someone or something else. After prayerfully choosing to own and affirm them for yourself,
surrender the past event or relationship to God to be blessed
and transformed into a Holy Relationship.

4. **Refill**: Now take 2-3 minutes to imagine drawing Light down
from the ethers, through your head, and into your heart for
the next several inhalations. At the same time, hear the words,
Love and *Healing* or *Peace* and *Joy*, or whatever two words you
prefer (which is commonly referred to as a mantra). Then, on
the exhalation, simply spread the energy throughout your body
as you hear the words, "And so it is."

5. **Give Thanks**: Lastly, prayerfully give thanks to God for the
healing, as well as thanking whoever popped up in your exercise, since they now have given you the opportunity to recognize a pattern wherein you had rejected your own goodness and

transferred it onto someone else. Also give thanks that you now have chosen to fill yourself with a greater abundance of God.

CHECKING-IN EXERCISE

One of the best, and simplest, exercises for improving communication is this "Checking-In Exercise," suggested by many couples' counselors. Similar to taking a pulse of ourselves, each other, and the relationship, this exercise (which only takes 10-20 minutes) helps couples to stay in touch with the condition of their relationship. Also, it offers a safe space wherein each person can be heard, and this alone can increase the couple's sense of value and safety with one another. Couples who take a regular pulse of their relationship by doing this Checking-In Exercise often find the benefits to be immeasurable.

1. After creating privacy with no possibility of interruptions, the couple (or group, family, etc.) sits facing one another.

2. The "rules of engagement" must be clearly established, which include not interrupting the person whose turn it is to speak.

3. Decide who goes first as the speaker and who first will be the listener.

4. Begin by briefly sharing something (or some things) you appreciate about each other or about any positive changes going on in the relationship.

5. Then share updates with each other, which can be any new insights, revelations, epiphanies, or anything that happens to be going on in your life—major or minor.

6. Share ideas about what changes might help the relationship grow to another level—including sharing any needs that might be helpful to have met.

7. Next, if it is agreeable, the silent person can now ask questions— as long as there are clear rules about what can be asked and exactly how honest the answers will be.

8. End by complimenting and extending thanks for everything that was shared/communicated and perhaps exchange an embrace.

9. Switch roles and allow the other person to have his or her turn, following the same rules.

RETIRING ROLES EXERCISE

This exercise assists couples (or any two people) in bringing closure to the past—old patterns, contracts, and roles that were once chosen or lived-out. The exercise helps us to be vulnerable enough to own what we have allowed others to project onto us, as well as owning what we have projected onto them. When the exercise is completed, both individuals usually feel a tremendous sense of release and relief. This sense of release and relief comes to us when we let go of the heavy burdens of illusion we have been carrying for others and have allowed them to carry for us. Cleansed of these burdens, we now have the space to start over and make healthier choices—even if we still choose to continue a relationship of some kind with this person.

1. Sit comfortably across from one another—holding hands (if that feels appropriate). Decide which person will share first. Then take a few centering breaths and look gently into each other's eyes.

2. The person chosen to share first should share with the other, something along these lines. [The words can vary based on the type of relationship, but this example is for couples.]

"I need to share some important feelings with you today. First of all, I want you to know that there are several things that I appreciate about you and about our relationship. [Insert examples.] I also want you to know how much I love you and how much I care about you. I wish for you all the best things in life and that all of your greatest dreams come true. I hope you know that I would love nothing more than to be able to ease all of your worries and remove all of your problems. I would love to be there every time you need someone and to be the most important person in your life. And it breaks my heart to say this, but we both need you to know that I cannot do all of these things for you. I would love to, but I can't. So today I am retiring myself from the role of trying to be everything for you. This means that it's possible that the person you once knew (as me) will no longer be that person. The person you knew was wearing several hats and several masks, but all of these now are being removed. So you may no longer like the person I am if I am no longer being someone for you. And, it is my hope that you will be interested in getting to know the new me, the real me. If you choose not to do so, I will understand—even if it hurts. But I would like you to take some time to think about it, and then let me know if you would like to get to know me as I now am getting to know myself. Thank you!"

3. The second person now repeats the same exact statement.

4. Lastly, the couple might relax, perhaps share a hug, and arrange themselves. They might then choose to share a few heartfelt words, or they might choose to simply remain silent for a while. Either way, they should commit to a time in the near future wherein they can share the answer to the final question

they each asked (whether or not their partner would like to get to know the new them, as they develop and get to know themselves).

ROLE-PLAY EXERCISE

The following exercise is fairly common for counselors and healers who use any form of "role playing" or "psycho-drama" as part of their regime for healing. The exercise can be done with a second person playing the role of our parent or partner (or anyone else with whom it would help to share our feelings). The exercise can also be done with the same person (client) playing both roles: the role of herself (or himself) and then switching chairs and playing the role of the other person. In either case, such as exercise can be deeply emotional, as well as offering very helpful insights into past and current relationships.

In the following instructions, "Person 1" represents the subject or client or recipient of the exercise and can be the subject as a child or adult or any age or role (such as husband or wife) that is needed. "Person 2" is played by a friend, healer, therapist, or even may be the second role of the client playing Person 1. The sample role play exercise below may change completely based on the reason for the exercise and the responses that emerge from each question or comment. Person 1 should ad lib as needed and allow emotions to arise and flow until it either feels complete *or* as though it is time to move on. Be sure to stay focused on the exercise and avoid getting side-tracked into casual conversation.

Person 1: To husband, wife, parents, etc… "I need to share my feelings about our life and relationship."
Person 2: "What do you need to say?"

Person 1: "My relationship with you affected (*or* affects *or* is affecting) my life. It affects my health, my self-worth, my parenting, my relationships, etc…"

Person 2: "What is it like to have been in a relationship with me?"

Person 1: *Share spontaneously what it was like to live with this person. Continue sharing until you feel complete.*

Person 2: "In what way did I most hurt you?"

Person 1: *Share reply until you feel complete.*

Person 2: "In what way did I most confuse you?"

Person 1: *Share reply until you feel complete.*

Person 2: "In what way did I most frustrate you?"

Person 1: *Share reply until you feel complete.*

Person 2: "In what way did I most make you sad?"

Person 1: *Share reply until you feel complete.*

Person 2: "What did you *want* most from me?"

Person 1: *Share reply until you feel complete.*

Person 2: "What did you most *get* from me, instead?"

Person 1: *Share reply until you feel complete.*

Person 2: "What do you most need now to create the healthiest life for yourself?"

Person 1: *Share reply until you feel complete.*

Person 2: "Anything I have done, was done not from my true self but from my wounded self and had nothing to do with you or your true value. I am sorry and I ask for and accept your forgiveness. Thank you."

Person 1: "It is time to release these issues and memories to a new level of healing. But to do that, I have to let *you* go." *Then person 1 visualizes person 2 fading away until gone (for about 30 seconds) as they both say goodbye 3 times.*

BUILDING CONNECTION
(hand-holding) EXERCISE

This is a simple, yet profound exercise that is best done in pairs. However, it can be done between two or more people—even a large group. This exercise helps develop our understanding of connection.

1. Face your partner and sit as close together as possible.

2. Hold each other's hand—right hand only—so that you are holding right hand to right hand (which can also be done left hand to left hand). Make sure you are not reaching too far, thus making yourself uncomfortable when sitting this way for several minutes. Also, rest the hands that are held together on one of the partner's lap or thigh.

3. Close your eyes and take a minute to connect with your breathing and begin centering in.

4. Calmly become aware of your own hand and everything about it. Be aware of whether your hand is on top or bottom; be aware of where your fingers are. Notice if they are curled or straight and which ones are more curled and which are straight. Even notice the temperature of the different parts of your hand. Think of nothing other than that hand—your hand—not your partner's.

5. Now do the same with your partner's hand: Can you picture your partner's hand? Do you know how curled the fingers are? Do you know exactly where the ring finger is? What about the nail of the middle finger? Where is it right now? Without looking, can you tell? That is pure concentration, pure presence... being nowhere else.

6. Next, bring your other hand in, until you can touch your partner's right hand with both of your hands. In this position, you

CREATING FULFILLING RELATIONSHIPS

are not having each of your two hands holding onto each of their two hands. Instead, you are having both of your hands on your partner's one, right hand and the same goes for your partner. Now use both hands to explore your partner's one hand just as you did with only one hand to one hand.

7. Once you are done exploring your partner's hand with both of your hands, gently pause and just hold your partner's hand, while your partner holds yours. Continue doing this for a minute or so, as you convey a feeling of gratitude for sharing the exercise.

8. Keeping your eyes closed, imagine that although there are several billion people on the planet, this is the person holding your hands, and whose hands you are holding. It cannot be an accident or coincidence. Somehow you both are sitting here, somehow drawn to this exercise. This is not to say that if you are strangers, you now must become friends or get married. But just feel grateful that out of all the people on the planet, this person chose to be here with you.

9. Become aware that the hands you are holding belong to a human being. With your mind, follow your partner's arms up to his or her heart center. Then consider the following: These hands have been with this person for a long time—his or her whole life. The hands you are holding have been clenched in pain, wiped away tears, held hands with loved ones, and waved goodbye. The hands you are holding have carried their first little lunch-box to school and climbed the monkey-bars. It's amazing! These hands and this person have been through so much—not always pleasant—not always difficult. And yet this person is allowing you to hold them in trust and care. And, in honor of this person, during the entire exercise, you were no-

where else but with them. That is what true connection is like. That is true intimacy and trust.

10. To conclude, give your partner's hands a gentle squeeze, as you convey (with your mind) a loving gratitude for everything that was just shared. Then, slowly open your eyes and, if you feel inspired to do so, exchange a hug with your partner.

WORKSHOP INTENSIVES

Offered by Michael Mirdad

There are three primary workshop intensives offered by Michael Mirdad. The first, in the spring, is Healing: Body and Soul and is designed to bring the attendees to new levels of physical, emotional, and spiritual health, while also teaching them how to become healers (or better healers). The second, in the summer, is Living Mastery. This workshop is great for anyone who is ready to discover new levels of direction, responsibility, balance, and wholeness. The third workshop, in the fall, Initiations Into Christ Consciousness, teaches attendees to connect with their True (Christ) Self and deeper levels of spiritual awareness.

HEALING: BODY & SOUL

This workshop is a 5-day intensive for anyone seeking to receive physical and/or emotional healing or choosing to develop greater healing abilities. It is perfect for those wanting to renew their commitment to maintaining physical/emotional health and spiritual connectedness and includes training in herbology, massage, energy work, Tai Chi, acupressure, Reiki, emotional healing, yoga, cranial release, health intuitiveness.

"I am so grateful that the workshop re-ignited or deepened the healer in me. I absolutely loved using a combination of breath work, physical body work, intuition, and advanced techniques to trigger issues on a cellular level to bring them forth to be healed. We learned healing and counseling skills that most counselors don't even know!" –Ron, ONT

LIVING MASTERY INTENSIVE

This workshop is a 5-day intensive for those who are prepared to live a life of fulfillment. It teaches how to experience the best life possible in every aspect of living. No other single event offers so much! Living Mastery is an advanced training for students and teachers of spirituality who are ready to learn how to manifest a spiritual, integrated, balanced, and prosperous life, as well as learning how to bring God and all spiritual learning into their daily lives and activities. Topics include the following: physical mastery–manifesting prosperity, living healthy through yoga and diet, and training in several healing arts; emotional mastery–developing psychic abilities, creating fulfilling relationships, and learning advanced emotional healing techniques; mental mastery–developing greater focus, learning effective meditation, and discovering your soul's purpose; and spiritual mastery–developing a life plan, learning true forgiveness, awakening higher levels of consciousness, and opening your heart center.

"I am so honored to have had the opportunity to experience five of the most amazing days of my life, while attending the Mastery Workshop. I became aware of my strength and endurance through rock climbing, yoga, and the obstacle course. I embraced exercises in past life regression and emotional healing. I was challenged doing exercises in cloud busting and learning the importance of focusing, as well as dividing and conquering life's obstacles. And I learned the importance of prayer and meditation and letting God live through me every instant of my life." –Janet, NY

www.GrailProductions.com

INITIATIONS INTO
CHRIST CONSCIOUSNESS

This workshop is an advanced training for students and teachers of Christ Consciousness. It covers advanced teachings and spiritual concepts, as well as profound levels of application. Attendees learn to clear their centers of consciousness and live a life that reflects their higher self in mind, body, and soul. This workshop also covers the following: initiations into Christ Consciousness through rarely understood mystery teachings of Jesus–some of which were transferred to Mary Magdalene, clearing of various energy centers (chakras), the secret teachings of Christ, Jesus' missing years amongst the Essenes and the Mystery Temples, and experiencing your own spiritual baptism.

"There were so many wonderful activities at this workshop. The information about the history of the universe was clear, informative and intriguing. The closing initiation into the Christ Consciousness was transformative. When I lay down in the middle of the circle, I felt the amplification of energy, all the light, in my body. As my heart chakra opened, I felt as if my entire chest were being pulled up to the ceiling, while my breath was deep and being pulled through my body to my feet. I felt like I was in the zone of Jesus, Mary, and of course fellow attendees. I feel as though I have attained a new spiritual level." –Jean, OR

www.GrailProductions.com

SACRED SITES JOURNEYS
With Michael Mirdad
THE INITIATORY JOURNEY

Since the beginning of time, students and masters on the spiritual path have taken journeys of initiation to sacred sites. These holy places included France, Egypt, Central America, and Britain. Initiates brought with them a sacred technology to build temples, megaliths, and ascension sites for healing and for harnessing the Earth's grid system.

Today these journeys still serve as a powerful ritual for personal power and spiritual awakening for planet Earth and all its inhabitants. Come and join us in this personal and planetary awakening.

SAMPLES OF SOME OF OUR JOURNEYS

FRANCE
Grotto-Home of Mary Magdalene
St. Marie de La Mer
Lourdes
Sacred Cathar & Templar Sites
France's Mount of St. Michael
IRELAND
Newgrange
Sacred Hill of Tara
Numerous Ancient Goddess Sites
SCOTLAND
Findhorn
Scottish Highlands
Magical Iona Island
Rosslyn Chapel

ENGLAND
Crop Circles
Avebury & Stonehenge
Glastonbury Abbey
The Chalice Well
Numerous Arthurian Sites
GREECE
Delphi
Legendary Islands
Athens
EGYPT
Great Pyramids
Valley of the Kings
Karnak
Temples of the Nile

Price includes: international travel from US and back, shared lodging, tour guides, most meals, entrance to sacred sites, teaching sessions, and more. Space is limited! Contact us now to register or to get on our mailing list.

Grail Productions PO Box 1908 • Sedona • AZ 86339
For information: 360-671-8349 or office@grailproductions.com
Visit us at **www.GrailProductions.com**

181

Other Books by Michael Mirdad

Healing the Heart & Soul $15.00

"Offering the essential ingredients for life transformation, this book provides deeper understanding as to why some people don't seem to heal, as well as the roles of forgiveness, mirroring, and miracles in relation to healing... it highlights key principles ... and presents them in a simple, accessible, and useful format."

–**Donna Eden,** *Energy Medicine*

The Seven Initiations on the Spiritual Path $15.00

"...an excellent portrayal of what each of us 'grows' through in reaching the goal of enlightenment. Michael Mirdad clearly explains the difference between learning the easy way or the hard way."
–**Rev. Jerry Bartholow,** *Peace Soup*

An Introduction to Tantra and Sacred Sexuality $15.00

"This is the first book in 20 years that I could wholeheartedly recommend. It should be on every bookshelf. Michael Mirdad speaks from his own rich experience, which is rare and is to be applauded."
–**David A. Ramsdale**
Sexual Energy Ecstacy

You're Not Going Crazy ... You're Just Waking Up! $15.00

"The leading edge of a new wave of books designed to help us achieve peace from the inside out as we make our way back to perfect oneness with God."

–**Gary R. Renard**
The Disappearance of the Universe

ORDER FORM

To order any of our books or request more information on any of these publications, please copy and mail in this order form or call our office or visit our website for a complete list of books, CDs, and DVDs.

Name_____

Address_____

City, State, Zip_____

Phone_____

Email_____

Make checks payable to: Grail Productions

OTHER BOOKS BY MICHAEL MIRDAD

An Introduction to Tantra and Sacred Sexuality
_____ copies at $15.00 each =   _____

Creating Fulfilling Relationships
_____ copies at $15.00 each =   _____

Healing the Heart & Soul
_____ copies at $15.00 each =   _____

Sacred Sexuality: A Manual for Living Bliss
_____ copies at $25.00 each =   _____

Seven Initiations on the Spiritual Path
_____ copies at $15.00 each =   _____

You're Not Going Crazy...You're Just Waking Up!
_____ copies at $15.00 each =   _____

Add $2.50 for S&H per book   _____

Total   _____

Grail Productions PO Box 1908 • Sedona • AZ 86339
For information: 360-671-8349 or office@grailproductions.com
Visit us at www.GrailProductions.com

About the Author

M ichael Mirdad is a world-renowned spiritual teacher, healer, and author. He has worked as a healer and spiritual counselor for over 30 years and is the author of the best-selling books *You're Not Going Crazy...You're Just Waking Up!*, *An Introduction to Tantra and Sacred Sexuality,* and *Healing the Heart & Soul.* Michael has facilitated thousands of classes, lectures, and workshops throughout the world on Mastery, Spirituality, Relationships, and Healing and is commonly referred to as a "teacher's teacher" and a "healer's healer."

Michael Mirdad has been featured as a keynote speaker in the world's largest expos and conferences and has been on radio, television, and various internet programs. His work has been published in several leading magazines including *Whole Self Times, Sedona Journal,* and *Yoga Journal,* as well as the cover feature in *Evolve* magazine. Michael Mirdad is respected as one of the finest and most diverse healers of our time and well-known for his ability to share the deepest teachings in a clear, applicable manner.